301.153
Hay
c. 1

Hayden
Rebellion and repression.

Glendale College
Library

I

Rebellion and Repression

BOOKS BY TOM HAYDEN
Rebellion in Newark
The Other Side
Rebellion and Repression

REBELLION
AND
REPRESSION

Testimony by **Tom Hayden**
before the National Commission
on the Causes and Prevention
of Violence, and the House
Un-American Activities
Committee

MERIDIAN BOOKS
THE WORLD PUBLISHING COMPANY
New York and Cleveland

301.153
Hay

A MERIDIAN BOOK

Published by The World Publishing Company
2231 West 110th Street, Cleveland, Ohio 44102
Published simultaneously in Canada
by Nelson, Foster & Scott Ltd.

First Printing—1969

Copyright © 1969 by The New Weekly Project, Inc.
All rights reserved. No part of this book
may be reproduced in any form without written
permission from the publisher, except for brief
passages included in a review appearing in a
newspaper or magazine.

Library of Congress Catalog Card Number: 72–98130
Printed in the United States of America

WORLD PUBLISHING
TIMES MIRROR

301,153
Hay

5351

A\7\

Preface

The events in the streets of Chicago during the Democratic National Convention in August, 1968, evoked a variety of responses from local and federal authorities. In two cases, committees of notables sought to investigate the disorders, assign causes, fix blame, and recommend punishments or preventives. One was the National Commission on the Causes and Prevention of Violence; the other was the House of Representatives' Committee on Un-American Activities. Both of them called Tom Hayden, a long-time organizer of radical action in the New Left of the Sixties, to testify—the Violence Commission by "invitation" and HUAC by subpoena. Hayden appeared before the Violence Commission on October 23, and before HUAC on December 2 and 3, 1968. Then, on March 21, 1969, he was indicted—along with seven others—by a Federal Grand Jury in Chicago for conspiring in planning the convention action.

The dramatis personae in the hearings are listed in their order of appearance in the transcripts that follow. Violence Commission: Thomas D. Barr, Deputy Director of the Commission; Dr. W. Walter Menninger, of the Menninger Clinic; Sen. Philip A. Hart, Democrat of Michigan; Leon Jaworski, a Houston lawyer and confidant of President Johnson; Milton S. Eisenhower, Chairman of the Commission; Albert E. Jenner, Jr., a Chicago lawyer; Judge A. Leon Higginbotham, of the Federal District Court in Philadelphia. HUAC: Frank Conley, special counsel to the Committee; Rep. Richard Ichord, Democrat of Michigan; Rep. John Ashbrook, Repub-

5

lican of Ohio; Rep. Albert Watson, Republican of South Carolina.

Both transcripts are "unofficial"; the texts have been slightly edited, to remove some redundant or extraneous material, and to give clarity to a few obscure exchanges. Excerpts from the HUAC testimony first appeared in the March 17–24, 1969, issue of *Hard Times* (formerly *Mayday*).

ANDREW KOPKIND
Editor, *Hard Times*

Contents

Introduction
by Tom Hayden

The black rebellions from Watts to Detroit, the youth rebellions from the Pentagon to Chicago, and the military successes of the Vietnamese are forcing an embarrassed U.S. power elite to look desperately for scapegoats. They have decided to put radicalism on trial.

Sometimes this trial is conducted violently and without due process, as in the shooting and gassing of people in the streets; sometimes the trial is carried on in the courtroom, as in the jailing of black revolutionaries, draft resisters, and soldiers protesting the war; and finally, the trial includes attempts to discredit the Movement in the eyes of the people. This last method is the one attempted by the two government agencies which held the hearings published in this book.

The House Un-American Activities Committee and the National Commission on Violence are two sides of the same coin of political persecution.

HUAC has adopted a new name—the House Internal Security Committee—to carry on its traditional harassment of radicals. In direct collaboration with the Chicago police and the FBI, HUAC is trying to demonstrate the existence of a subversive and terrorist plot to burn down Chicago last summer.

HUAC represents such a stupid and discredited approach, however, that the need has arisen for a more "respectable" group of inquisitors. The Violence Commissioners are ideal. First, they created an image of "objectivity" by issuing (without actually endorsing) the famous Walker Report on Chicago, which concluded that the police "rioted" after being "provoked" by the demonstrators. By blaming individual policemen, the Walker Report covered up the real conspirators who gave the police their orders in Chicago: Daley, Hum-

GLENDALE COLLEGE LIBRARY

phrey, Johnson. By blaming us for "provocation" (consisting mainly of our insulting language and appearance), the Walker Report contributed directly to the climate in which eight of us were indicted for conspiracy to incite a riot. In addition, the commission investigators have turned over their reports on many campus radicals to the Pentagon's counter-insurgency department.

Why testify before such inquisitors? Not to testify before HUAC would invite a "contempt of Congress" indictment. Not to testify before the Violence Commission, after being invited, would imply that revolutionaries are intransigent, opposed to "dialogue," and have something to hide. The problem, then, was to use their own forum to ridicule their authority, defy their stereotypes, and present a meaningful case to the American people.

The public is the final jury in this trial, and the public does not know what to think. As Eldridge Cleaver says, "The basic problem in this country today is political confusion. People don't know whether to be afraid of the right or the left. They don't know whether they themselves belong on the right or on the left, so they just say, fuck it, throw up both hands, take acid trips, freak out on weed and pills—alcohol is still with us—people feel that they just can't deal with the situation. And that's because, I believe, the people have been consciously manipulated to that end."

The people are being told that their enemies are the "extremists"—black and brown, students and hippies. The people are being barraged with reactionary propaganda. The universities are hopelessly dependent on Defense Department contracts, yet when blacks at Cornell arm themselves against threatened attacks, *Newsweek* runs the headline: "Universities Under the Gun." The trustees of every school in America represent the business elite, yet the Attorney General accuses radicals of imposing a "minority tyranny on the nation's campuses." The Attorney General's top assistant calls the Left "ideological criminals" who should be rounded up in detention camps. These people express the most genocidal policies since Hitler, yet they denounce the New Left as "Nazi storm troopers."

The truth is that we all live under a system which requires violence because it is based on the exploitation of man by man. America was founded in genocidal wars with the Indians and the Mexicans. America created the most brutal system of slavery in the Western Hemisphere, killing 50 million people along the way. America was industrialized through the savage exploitation of the working class. Every democratic reform in American history has been achieved only after bloodshed and disruption—from the Boston Tea Party to the Revolutionary War, the Civil War, the women's suffrage movement, the unionizing of farmers and industrial workers. This system of capitalism and racism causes massive violence not only inside our nation's borders but everywhere in the world where it tries to impose itself. Nobody in the world is safe from the "ugly Americans" who come to take their land, their resources, and their cultural identities. Wars like Vietnam are a logical result of the drive for world domination by the American establishment.

Against this backdrop, the "violence of the Left" is minor. Our total violence over the last five years has not reached that of a single B-52 raid in Vietnam.

Our rulers know this, yet they persist in claiming we are the chief cause of "disorder" in America. The rulers have to take this sorry position in order to cover up an even sorrier one. They are on the defensive, they and their authority are being questioned and exposed by more people every day. How indeed can these characters explain themselves? They obviously cannot tell the truth about their intentions. What would they say? That blacks must suffer longer because whites are a superior race? That the Vietnamese should be slaughtered because the United States must control Asia? That rotten education should be perpetuated because the power structure needs a class of robots at its disposal? This power structure is bankrupt. Having no solutions to the pressing economic and social needs of people, they must think of an excuse.

So the rulers these days acknowledge in public that "change" and "reform" are needed, but their excuse is that "law and order" must be secured first. The chief obstacle to "change," according to Establishment propaganda, is the very movement which demanded the change in the first place. Those who originally demanded the changes are being shot down, jailed, or kicked out of school.

Who are they kidding? Are we expected to believe that Richard Nixon, the number one empty-headed conformist of our time, suddenly has become a social reformer? That if we stop "shouting," as requested in his Inaugural Address, we can trust him to deal with people's desperate needs?

Richard Nixon lacks even the faintest capacity to understand human need. That is why he is turning over the government to the police.

But the more our country is controlled by a police state, the more discontent will grow. A police state means: thought control, wage and price control, antistrike regulations, political persecution, endless chaos. Instead of taking our "great society" to Asia, as Hubert Humphrey once promised, we are bringing Vietnam home. We are creating an America where it is necessary for the government to rule behind barbed wire, for the President to speak only at military bases, and where, finally, it will be necessary for the people to fight back.

The only way there could be "peace" in such an America would be for millions of people to accept their own enslavement. But too many of us are insisting on the right to own our own minds, to think for ourselves, to live as human beings.

For our movement, the present level of rebellion and repression requires several new points of departure.

1. We must emphasize that the government is taking *politi-*

cal prisoners, and reject the rulers' definition that we are "law-breakers." We must make the issue of repression a basic one while still continuing the battle against the war, against racism, against the universities, which are the causes of the repression.

2. We have to take care of our political prisoners. A few of us have ample publicity and competent lawyers, but thousands of people are in jail or facing jail alone. We need machinery to organize support for the many unknown prisoners. If we give them a feeling that their sacrifice is worthwhile, they will project courage back from their cells to strengthen those on the outside.

3. We need to expand our struggle to include a total attack on the courts. The court system is just another part of this rigged apparatus that is passed off as "open and impartial." The system is most threadbare within the military and municipal courts, but can be exposed at all levels. There is no reason for us to become submissive at the courtroom door.

4. The people are the jury. We will win our particular cases as well as the general struggle not by appeals to the Supreme Court or by "deals" with prosecutors but by taking the issues over and over to the public. The power to keep our movement free resides only in the people.

5. We must become more international. We must break America's ability to project a democratic and stable image to the world. For the dual purpose of fighting repression and making total change, we must work together with those who are fighting to remove American capitalists and militarists from their soil: Not only Third World liberation fighters, but all those in Western Europe who will picket embassies and create sanctuary for deserters, for Eldridge and others.

6. We should stand on the right to self-defense and revolution as protected by the Bill of Rights and Declaration of Independence. We should not let the rulers dishonor these fundamental rights by persecuting us. We cannot avoid con-

frontation, but we can choose the issues and the battleground. The power structure will become more and more violent. Even if we beat them in their own rigged courts, they will then create "courts" of their own to take care of us. We have to be able to survive, to fight back against whatever level of terror or coercion is applied. The coming of repression will speed up time, making a revolutionary situation—especially between the power structure and the black colony—more likely. If we look at the last ten years, we see that history is moving faster and calling us to become a new generation of American revolutionaries.

7. We must combine our separate movements into a united revolutionary front to combat and survive repression, and to develop a common program for revolutionary change. The more repressive the power structure becomes, the more it neglects the needs of the whole people. Repression means a threat to the Movement, but also an opportunity to provide an alternative to the people who are confused.

We have to give up any illusions about "peaceful" and "legal" methods of change working in the long (and perhaps even the short) run. Repression cannot be avoided. The question is whether repression will succeed in isolating our movement, creating fear among the people, and tangling us in defensive battles, or whether the repression will work against itself, outraging and educating the people, expanding the Movement, leading to continued offensive action against the Establishment. The case of Huey Newton has hurt the police and helped the Panthers. The "not guilty" verdict of the Oakland Seven (who led demonstrations at the induction center in 1967) was a great embarrassment to the prosecutors. The army trials of the twenty-seven Presidio "mutineers" are outraging GIs and the entire public. Each case of this kind traps the Establishment in a dilemma: If they crack down, they cause great public criticism; if they do not crack down, the rebels remain on the loose.

Whether repression works depends basically on our spirit. If we are cautious or paranoid, if we focus only on our own defense and forget the issues that made us originally rebel, our feelings will spread and weaken the morale of the people. If we keep a fighting spirit, and define the issues over and over, the people will support us as their warriors.

Berkeley, California
June, 1969

Part One

HAYDEN: First of all, I should say very frankly that I don't come here with any expectation of a dialogue or understanding being achieved or with any belief in the legitimacy of the commission. Frankly, I think that it is very difficult for a person in my position to believe that you are actually prepared to study the real causes of violence as I see them in the country. There are no young people on the commission, no student activists, no draft resisters, no outspoken critics of the draft.

At the time of the commission's creation, I recall in the press certain reports that certain commissioners felt there was a link between the assassination of Senator Kennedy and ghetto rebellions and campus rebellions. This would be a good case of the criminal calling the victim to task for the crime, if this were your way of thinking. The way in which this kind of distortion seems to be achieved is by using national martyrs for purposes which are exactly contrary to what they stood for in their life.

For example, the assassination of Dr. King was followed by the passage of a meaningless housing law coupled with a very meaningful and very repressive antiriot statute. Now after the assassination of Senator Kennedy, your commission is created which studies the antiwar protest movement rather than studying the slaughter in Vietnam and the white racism which Robert Kennedy had the courage to criticize in his life.

Much as I politically or personally may have disagreed with Senator Kennedy, my personal opinion is he would have regarded the focus of this commission as an insult to what he stood for. My only purposes for coming here, therefore, are twofold, and they have to do with simply stating for the official record, first, that the sources of violence in this country are to be found in the war on Vietnam which you should be studying rather than in student protest movements, draft resistance, or the antiwar movement. And in a deeper sense violence in this country stems from a system which is sick, which is racist, which apparently has a boundless ambition to police the world, which is therefore losing authority and legitimacy in the eyes of millions of young people in this country and many millions more of people around the world, a system which relies more and more on the use of force, on the use of police to maintain itself rather than relying on consent or persuasion or traditional techniques of democracy.

The second statement that I would like to make is that the antiwar movement, the draft resistance movement is not a nihilistic handful of true believers, that our position is composed of actual human beings with actual needs that we believe are denied, illegally and immorally denied. This solution to the war cannot be pacified with trick solutions, nor will it be eliminated through repression, because the opposition is composed of people who do not want to die or live in constant disorder, but who will not become "good Germans" quietly accepting an insane, immoral order of things. There is nothing sinister or incomprehensible about the opposition, about young people, about students in this country, except to their enemies who think their own authority is beyond question and challenge.

The New Left in this country has been very reluctant to become revolutionary. Like many young people at that time, I was given a good deal of hope by the 1960 presidential campaign of Sen. John Kennedy and particularly by the Peace Corps. I felt, and many other young people at the time felt, that the Cold War and the arms race were not only suicidal in their long-run implications but poisonous to a democratic system because of the necessary creation of stereotypes, the anti-Communist obsession that was involved, the growth of the military-industrial complex. So for many of us, the Peace

Corps represented an alternative symbolically, a way out of the Cold War: and at the same time, an alternative to the rat-race careers that most young people faced unhappily. But our initial enthusiasm melted almost before the first Peace Corps volunteers went overseas. Many of the most creative volunteers were given trouble by administrators or sent home or identified by their bosses as misfits. We have heard that label from authorities before—misfits—all through high school and college and from our parents.

We saw the Peace Corps become wedded to American foreign policy as a whole. Its more decent programs we saw represented essentially ways to brighten up the more brutal and exploitative patterns of American foreign policy, an attempt to show people in the Third World an American idealism that in effect was muzzled and ineffective.

We dropped out rather quickly from the Peace Corps and as you know today it is the opposite of its original conception. It is facing immense recruiting problems because of disinterest and hostility on American campuses.

The major issue that shaped our political outlook, however, was not foreign policy and the issue of the Peace Corps, but it was domestic policy and particularly the problem of civil rights in the South, which came to the attention of Northern students in 1960 through the direct action of voter-registration campaigns. In these campaigns white middle-class students like myself went South with a confidence that the conscience of the United States of America was on our side. Working in the South brought us face to face for the first time with the reality that we had never known, the direct reality of the police state. Civil-rights workers were arrested by the thousands, beaten by the hundreds, killed on one occasion, or terrorized by policemen constantly. The crucial discovery of that experience for many students, however, was that the South was not an isolated and backward region but was an integral part of the whole country. We found that the Justice Department

would move neither fast enough nor with sufficient forceful-
ness to protect people conducting sit-ins or voter registration.
No legal reasons were given for this slowness or lack of force-
fulness. We realized that political reasons were fundamental.
The federal government and Democratic Party could not and
would not offend Southern officials.

An elementary lesson began to dawn on us, a lesson that
never was taught us in our civics classes, and that lesson was
simply that law serves power. Law serves power. So, despite
the literal meaning of the Declaration of Independence and
the Constitution, the South would remain segregated, and to
take just one example, the Kennedy administration would
nominate segregationist judges to guarantee to the South an
acceptable administration of the law.

These lessons were deepened by the outbreak of rebellions
in Northern cities after 1964. Prior to these outbreaks, conventional wisdom declared to us that the racial problem was basically a regional one, that the North was more liberal than the
South, but the rebellions laid bare to white students that the
reality of the North was no different in substance from that of
the South.

City government and its agencies are more oppressive than
they are representative institutions for people in the ghettos.
There is no community machinery for control of the police,
the landlord, the merchant, the social worker, or other para-
sitic elements which patrol and exploit the ghetto. The rebellions, looked upon this way, were a rational response to this
system of exploitation. They involved more people than any
civil-rights demonstrations which petitioned authorities. Their
targets were not unstructured but were precise. The targets
were the symbols of oppression, particularly of the stores in
the ghetto. Although masses of apparently unorganized people were in the streets, there was little violence against white
people, although thousands of blacks were injured, hundreds
were killed. But the white community—from the suburbs to

24

the governmental offices—described the rebellions as disorders, riots, nihilism, and responded essentially with police and troopers. Because of their control of the mass media, they could create their own self-serving definitions of what these rebellions were all about. But any student who had been in the South could see that the sources of violence were different. The sources were in a racist system which, whatever its proclamations, so long as it remains racist cannot create justice for its victims and therefore needs military force to maintain itself.

When the victims rebel, greater force is employed to restore the status quo. People are arrested, beaten, and even shot down for supposedly stealing from stores which had illegally robbed them with the permission of the state for years. The law serves power.

In Vietnam we saw an international dimension to the violence and racism we were already seeing at home. I want to remind the commission that the antiwar movement began with the premise and with the expectation that Vietnam was a mistake which could be brought to the attention of the government, that legal and conventional channels were available which could be used.

I think that you will recall that we supported the peace candidate Lyndon B. Johnson in 1964 and thought that the most traditional weapon of democracy, the national election, produced a clear mandate for no further escalation of the war in Vietnam, a mandate which was overturned as quickly as the new administration settled in office.

I think you will remember that our protest marches, our teach-ins, and all of our initial activities involved the same premise. For example, when the teach-ins began in 1965, they were based on the concept of a dialogue which we thought, mistakenly in retrospect, could be achieved with the Department of State. Our foreign-policy officials were invited to universities. They participated in these teach-ins. The reason that they don't go to the major universities anymore is not because we have run them away, but because they know they have nothing to say, they know they would be defeated if they engaged in the democratic process of dialogue and discussion. So, they stay away out of embarrassment.

Even with regard to the draft, the antiwar movement, in respect to the war as a whole, took the position that the United States government was acting in basically an unconstitutional and illegal way. The illegality of the war consisted in its being fought without Congressional authorization, in violation of the Geneva Agreements and the United Nations Charter, and in a manner which violates agreements governing the rules of warfare to which the United States is a party.

The question of the war's illegality blends into a deeper problem for us, however, and that is the problem of the undemocratic way in which decisions have been made regarding the war all along. It is perfectly correct to say that these decisions are made by a small presidential circle that meets on Tuesdays for lunch at the White House, rather than by the Congress, but such a criticism at this time in our judgment does not go far enough. The constitutional crisis revealed by the war in Vietnam does not simply stem from the fact that the war is undeclared, that the war is Congressionally unauthorized. Therefore, the constitutional crisis would not be solved by a declaration of war. The crisis lies in the fact that foreign-policy decisions as a whole including those about Vietnam are made essentially without the democratic participation of the American people in a system which was really never set up to democratically involve people in foreign policy. Agencies such as the Pentagon, the armed services, the intelligence operations, defense contractors, and private investors, that is, the key agencies which determine foreign policy, are essentially private and independent bureaucracies shielded from, and secret from, the public. They control, by and large, the information which the American people receive. They interfere in the internal politics of other nations without the knowledge of the American public. They obtain and invest billions of dollars for their own purposes without public accountability.

Elected senators and congressmen cannot be thought of as a serious countervailing force against this foreign-policy establishment because, in the first place, elected officials come and go while these bureaucracies involve permanent machinery; in the second place, because elected officials have neither the means nor the resources to investigate this empire; and in the third place, because in order to win and remain in office, most elected officials need, to some degree, the support of this private establishment, and so they become its handmaidens rather than its public watchdogs.

Now, I think we should remind ourselves that in spite of all difficulties that I have described in using regular channels, the antiwar movement has succeeded remarkably even within the terms of a system which I think is rigged. Over one-third of American adults polled, and certainly a higher percentage of people under twenty-one who, of course, are not polled, are opposed to U.S. policies in Vietnam. There is no active support for the war, active organized public support comparable to the activity of the antiwar movement. A president of the United States has thought it in his best interest to voluntarily depose himself because of public pressure. The vast majority of students are opposed to this war, as shown by *Time* magazine's 1968 survey which showed McCarthy and Kennedy leading all hawk candidates by enormous margins.

In addition to this domestic discontent, which is measurable, it is clear that the majority of nations—that organized public opinion in the world—considers the United States to be the basic party at fault in Vietnam. Opinion polls in countries as diverse as Sweden, France, Brazil, and Mexico have shown enormous support for American withdrawal from Vietnam.

U Thant was not whistling in the dark when he said that a motion proposed to stop the bombing of North Vietnam, in the General Assembly of the United Nations, an Assembly which does not include China, North Korea, or North Vietnam or the National Liberation Front of South Vietnam, would be supported by a majority of the assembled nations.

Look at the situation of a student facing this problem. He has no vote. His voice does not count in the democratic manner. Attempts to work within the system have been frustrated, and a student is not able to avoid the war for two basic reasons in particular, two basic ways in which the war is brought to him: first, the draft, and second, the transformation of the university into an instrument of American foreign policy, including policy in Vietnam. For many students, the draft represents the most tangible form of oppression that they have experienced in their sheltered, middle-class lives.

Originally, the protest against the draft came from the protest against the war. But the more that students understood the draft, the more they realized that they had two objections to it. First of all, through the draft the American state interferes with what the students consider to be an inalienable right, the right of the individual to decide what he will die for. Second, the draft, we see, is an instrument of social management and manipulation. In the words of Selective Service documents, official documents, called "A Memorandum on Channeling," the draft and the deferment system are used to keep students working in acceptable careers, acceptable to the makers of the war and to the government of the United States. It is not primarily or exclusively used to supply manpower for wars but is used as a device to regulate the ambitions of American youth according to a national interest defined by men for whom the youth can only fight but not vote.

If you want that memorandum, I will submit it to you. You cannot get it any longer from the Selective Service because it caused great embarrassment when it was obtained from them and widely reprinted on campuses in 1965.

The experiences of students in the universities provided still more evidence that youth is seen by their elders as a social group to be feared, to be manipulated and channeled.

The first years of student protest, as you know, centered on the question of whether education was relevant to our lives, centered on the question of authoritarian administrations laying down rules about student housing and off-campus activities, but as the Vietnam war developed, we began to understand the university system in a different way.

No longer could we criticize it for being an ivory tower, because we began to see that the university itself was a key part of the machinery of violence that was being used in Vietnam.

Our own professors were using their so-called academic freedom to perfect methods of torture, methods of chemical and biological warfare. The Department of Defense was financing endless studies of how to defeat guerrillas and revolutionaries.

The National Student Association was revealed to be a secret front for the international activities of the CIA. From the viewpoint of America's rulers, apparently, the universities are indispensable to the modern military effort, and students must be conditioned to accept the status quo and trained to carry it on. Our conclusion was inescapable: to resist this attempt to absorb students and university resources into the military apparatus. To accept the university's status quo was to accept complicity in the violence in Vietnam.

So, what I am saying is that the student movement, the antiwar movement, was becoming more radical basically because of its experience in this society. From a position of expecting idealistically that authorities would listen to us, we were moving towards questioning the legitimacy of the authority.

Having tried available channels and discovered them meaningless, having recognized that the establishment does not listen to public opinion—it does not care to listen to the New Left—the New Left was moving toward confrontation.

The turning point, in my opinion, was October, 1967, when resistance became the official watchword of the antiwar movement.

We asserted that those who were involved in war crimes in Vietnam, those who had never been responsive to our conventional protest, those who turned a deaf ear to international public opinion had no right to continue their activities with immunity. We were not going to interrupt the right to talk because their talking was one of the best ways that our movement was organized. If they wanted to advocate illegal, criminal, inhuman activities, we would listen. We would let others listen.

Perhaps we would walk out of their lectures. Perhaps we would heckle them. Perhaps we would ask them embarrassing questions. Perhaps we would surround them later and boo.

They can advocate inhuman activities if that is all they could find to do. But as for those people connected with Dow Chemical Company, the U.S. Marine Corps, or the Central Intelligence Agency, who were recruiting on campuses, in our opinion they were not exercising free speech when they were recruiting. Free speech was one thing. Recruiting was something altogether different.

Just as butchers who sell poisoned meat should be closed down by their customers if the government does not put them in jail, so we felt that people who are recruiting for illegal and immoral activities—engaged in illegal and immoral business —should be stopped—should be stopped—and have no right to expect immunity on the campus while they go about their manufacture of napalm and their recruitment.

Just as the Nazis had no right to expect that people would sit by giving them immunity when they constructed gas chambers, the people who make napalm have no right to expect that people will sit by and grant them immunity in the manufacture of these weapons of war.

The only place at which we acted "illegally," if you want to call it that, for instance in the blocking of doors, was when we were attempting to create a response from a system which ignored our numbers and our words.

To say that we were acting illegally is to say that the manufacturer of napalm is legal, that the war in Vietnam is legal, that the system is operating according to law—much more according to law than those who block doors at universities.

We couldn't accept that. That was the beginning of a new stage into which the movement passed—to a concept of resistance against an inhuman and unresponsive machine. We were going beyond that form of civil disobedience in which the individual breaks the law to test its legality and then accepts the legitimacy of being punished and sent to jail.

We no longer believed and we do not believe that we should be punished by immoral, illegal, unconstitutionally constituted authorities for doing what is right.

The Columbia strike was the most visible expression of this new consciousness in the movement. For several years, students and community groups protested the construction of what they considered to be a segregated gymnasium and the slum-landlord role of the university in Harlem, all of which is illegal.

For over a year students protested Columbia's connection with the Institute for Defense Analyses, which is engaged in activities which we considered to be in violation of national and international law.

31

And Columbia engaged in secret research, secret research that by definition cannot be protested because you cannot find out in all cases what the research is about.

Yet the administration ruled the campus with typical arbitrary power. There existed at Columbia no effective democratic machinery for the students or even for the faculty (who had less rights than workers unionized in a factory) to express their will and to change policy.

Everyone was governed by trustees with lifetime terms, representing the major business and military interests that the students opposed. In this situation the students decided finally to occupy buildings. That action was termed illegal, but that term assumed the legitimacy of the authoritarian university power structure which allowed no other method of successful protest.

The students were called nihilistic but the atmosphere in the buildings was communal and disciplined. Students were said to be interfering with education, but they created, in their opinion, a freer university than Columbia ever was before.

Students were accused of destroying property. That is true only of doorknobs and some tables. But the police—and we have films, photographs, tapes, and observers who were hidden in the buildings to watch—the police systematically destroyed far more property after removing the strikers from the buildings, so as to be able to call our strike violent and nihilistic.

The overwhelming brutality in the Columbia situation came from the boots and the clubs of policemen. Now, at the same time that Columbia was going on and demonstrating the profound disillusionment of the student movement, something else was happening.

That was the 1968 election, and particularly the campaigns of Senator McCarthy and Senator Kennedy. With those campaigns a last hope was rekindled among some young people in the possibilities of working within the Establishment. This was especially true of the newer generations of students who agreed with the New Left in its opposition to the war and to racism but who had not yet been quite disillusioned enough by the police in the South and the other experiences that I have referred to, and so wanted to give electoral politics a chance.

For these young idealists who resembled, I think, in many ways the original Peace Corps volunteers who are of my generation, the campaign was a critical test of whether democracy could work.

Indeed, both Kennedy and McCarthy defined their campaigns as channels where youth could overcome their alienation while at the same time effectively exercising their power.

So, seen from that angle, the fate of Robert Kennedy and the defeat of Eugene McCarthy perhaps have caused a more rapid disillusionment for youth in this country than any other event of the 1960s.

Kennedy's death convinced young people that America as a whole society is irrational and off its bearings. McCarthy's defeat convinced young people that the political machinery is corrupt and insensitive, unrepresentative, and probably impossible to reform.

The sorry climax of this was the Democratic convention which apparently I cannot describe because a federal grand jury is preparing a case against us at the present time.

But I will only say that Chicago was only the most recent and blatant case of the criminal blaming the victim for the crime. And I will go no further.

In conclusion, our basic crime is not a disregard for law or an involvement in violence. The violence of our movement has been minimal, almost nonexistent, especially in comparison with the violence of other movements.

Let us discuss momentarily the labor movement. I will refer indirectly to Chicago. Just before Chicago and the convention occurred, electrical workers in Chicago took guns and shot down the electrical cables leading to the Nike site on the shore of Lake Michigan, thus exposing the citizens of Chicago to the possibility of a Soviet missile attack, I suppose: thus doing far more to aid the Communist cause than anyone who was coming to protest the convention; thus doing something more violent than any students at Chicago were accused of doing; because shooting down Nike cables is quite different from throwing a bag of urine at a policeman.

Yet this made second- or third-page news. It drew no great police investigation, no federal grand jury is examining this great threat to the American system that was imposed by shooting these cables.

It illustrates to me what we are accused of has to do with our political philosophy rather than with our supposedly disruptive and militant tactics, because I believe that our political philosophy is in conformity with reality as young people see it. And, therefore, if peaceful means were available, we would in the next generation be able to achieve a majority of the people who are presently young in this country to come around to our program.

Therefore, it is necessary to rewrite the rules of the game, to change the machinery, and to introduce violence to stop this and to try to turn attention away from our ideas and our political philosophy, which is basically democratic, and turn your attention to our tactics.

What we are essentially accused of, and what we are regarded as criminals for, has nothing essentially to do with our tactics. It has to do with the fact that we disrespect your authority. You cannot stand it.

It is true that we do call policemen pigs. It is true that we shout "fuck you LBJ" on the president's birthday. It is true that people take dope. It is true that people wore old clothes. It is true that people laughed at delegates. It is true that people climbed on the statues in Mayor Daley's park.

But it was our identity itself which was forbidden in Chicago and is forbidden in this society—unless you believe that any of these things constitute violations of law or constitute violations of order.

Our identity as a generation is what is becoming criminal in your eyes, and your laws are merely convenient devices to punish and exterminate that identity.

BARR: I take it that we agree, Mr. Hayden, that the purpose of any act of protest or demonstration is to win the support of the uncommitted majority, is that so?

HAYDEN: That is a goal.

BARR: The principal one?

HAYDEN: Well, a principal goal in Nazi Germany might have been to remove the Nazis from power by any means necessary, regardless of whether you had majority support or not. The goal in the American revolution, which was not a majority revolution—the American revolution which was carried out by a minority—was to remove the British presence from the United States. If you will agree with me that in some cases like the ones I have named there can be other goals, I will certainly agree with you, the primary goal where possible is the goal that you have stated.

BARR: I will accept that and will amend the question accordingly. Let's suppose that in a university context we are talking about adherence of the majority of the faculty, a majority of the students; in a broader context we are talking about the adherence of the general public.

Let us suppose that the majority, taking the university context, the majority of the faculty and students or the public, don't support the objectives now, the objectives of protest, and assume that this is so, assume that they do not, assume that they fully understand what the issues are all about, the relationships of one issue to another, that they are fully informed, and that they choose other objectives than those of the protesters, and assume also that the protesters seize build-

35

ings or block streets or forcibly interfere with the operation of the university. My question to you is what should the response of the university be or the society to these kinds of tactics by a minority group where the majority has clearly decided in favor of other objectives?

HAYDEN: Could you give me an example, say, at Columbia where that was true?

BARR: I want you to assume that it was true at Columbia. Let us assume that a majority of the students and a majority of the faculty members were opposed to the objectives of the SDS at Columbia.

HAYDEN: That is the assumption that I was going to contest, because if they were fully informed and fully aware, there would be no need for the contest.

BARR: I am asking you to make the assumption with me for the purpose of this argument, neither one of us will argue or concede that it is true or untrue, but assume that at Columbia, which may or may not be true, assume that the majority of the faculty and students were in favor of locating the gymnasium precisely where it was and precisely under the circumstances proposed, assume also that the research that was being carried on for the Institute of Defense Analyses was understood and approved by the majority of the students and a majority of the faculty, and assume the tactics—assume that what happened at Columbia did in fact happen, I want to put you in the role of administrator of the university. What would you do?

HAYDEN: Just put me there. Just put me there.

MENNINGER: The ultimate of your objective is to be in that seat?

BARR: Put yourself there. How would you respond to the situation?

HAYDEN: The situation that you are describing I would think of as similar to Nazi Germany, where the majority of the German people were uninformed about what was going on in

36

support of their government and that therefore anyone who could resist the policies of that government would have to also resist the tendencies of the majority in hopes of waking up that majority or changing that majority's mind and would have to face punishment, a physical kind, or be put in jail. That does not mean that you have to accept the administration or the punishment or the majority as being moral or legitimate in that kind of situation.

BARR: I am asking you a somewhat different question. Let's put you back in the role of the administrator. It sometimes helps us for analysis to reverse our roles. Let me be the student. Suppose that you were the administrator of a university, that you believed that a majority—

HAYDEN: I am Hitler—

BARR: You are the administrator of a free and open university.

HAYDEN: Which does research for Vietnam.

BARR: Which does whatever you think it ought to do.

HAYDEN: There is no such university.

BARR: Can you conceive of such a university being created?

HAYDEN: Yes.

BARR: If you will with me, assume that your conception has come to pass, then you were the head of the university—

HAYDEN: Then we would not have the problems that you are raising.

BARR: Your assumption, then, is, I take it, basically this: That the majority of the people agree with you and that the majority's will has to be implemented? Is that your basic position?

HAYDEN: No, no. Putting me in the position of Grayson Kirk is absurd because if I were he, it would be in my interest to do exactly what he did, which was to crack down on the students.

So it is very difficult to answer the question without saying I would have to violate my interest as a university administrator, because the interest of a university administrator today is in the control, regulation, and channeling of the students.

So I can't answer the question. On the question of majorities, the concept of majority is thrown around most blatantly by the president of the United States who said at first that his policy in Vietnam was justified because the opposition to it was only a handful of people, and he warned Hanoi not to get any false ideas about the size of the protest movement which he said was a scant minority. That was in '65. We were a scant minority.

In 1967 President Johnson says that he is like Winston Churchill, it doesn't matter whether a majority supports his policy, he will continue the war in Vietnam regardless of the majority will and be justified by history like Churchill was.

He even said if public support of the war was down to 1 percent, the war would go on.

I disagree with President Johnson about a lot of things, but I do agree that a man should stick to his guns and stick to his opinions even if 99 percent of the people disagree with him. The only thing is he should be removed from power at that point.

BARR: I take it you would also say if the opposition to the war in Vietnam dropped down to 1 percent and you were in that 1 percent, that the opposition ought to continue and you ought to also believe that he should be removed from power, even though you are in the 1 percent?

HAYDEN: I would believe that, but I would have no means to carry it out except to try to raise it with the 99 percent and organize them for that purpose. That already has been accomplished. People have been organized and he has been removed.

BARR: If we assume that you had failed as the 1 percent in organizing a majority of the other 99 percent, assume that with me, if you will, so we can get to the problem, and also assume with me that in the protest that you are engaged in, the process of seizing buildings and blocking streets and so on—what should the response be of the government which represents 99 percent of the people to your demonstrations? Should we permit them, encourage them, repress them? How should they respond to them?

HAYDEN: If they had 99 percent of the people, they would not even have to pay attention to it, because if your protest—

BARR: You have to pay attention to people that block streets. You have to respond to them in some way.

HAYDEN: Not as a government you don't. If 99 percent of the people agree with you, they will simply remove them. That is aside. There are two points I am trying to make in reference to your question. First of all, the individual—I think you will agree with this, it is fully within the American tradition—that an individual no matter how small a minority he represents ultimately has, as a matter of conscience, the right to resist and take any penalty that he receives as a result. He has that right. Secondly, to get back to reality, the students—

BARR: I would say you have that obligation.

HAYDEN: —the antiwar movement, the political organizations like SDS, just from a matter of realistically analyzing the situation, don't act in that way in the first place. That is why you are raising an unreal problem. The tactics of our movement are never to go so far as to try to alienate a majority of the people we are trying to organize. We may want to alienate you, we may want to alienate the press for our purposes, but we would certainly never move in a community or on a campus where we thought that the public feeling and popular feeling among our own people was going to be against it. So, the question would not come up. The occupation of those buildings only works because it has support on the Columbia campus. It only works because of that. You can see after Columbia, where students tried it, on other campuses because they wanted to mimic Columbia, and they did it without paying attention to the local atmosphere, they failed. Thirteen students run into an administration building; 700 do not follow, there is not enough of a legal problem to pay attention to. You can let a broom wielder or the night watchman or you can let the jocks in a fraternity come in and handle it.

BARR: As president of the university, would you say you ought to give it to the jocks to clean it out, or how would you, as a president, respond to it?

HAYDEN: How would I respond to thirteen people?

BARR: Thirteen people come in and seize your office, do you call in the jocks?

HAYDEN: If I were really smart, which university administrators never are, because they do not know how to save themselves, I would leave my office. I would organize a student rally and have the problems discussed at it. I would give my own opinions. I would have a referendum on the issues raised by the thirteen students. I would invite the press to go to my office and see what the thirteen students were doing in it. I would just let the situation drag itself out and win public support for my position by the most ruthlessly nonviolent methods possible.

HART: At the risk of offending some of my colleagues and you, I don't want my silence with respect to everything you have said to indicate that I agree with it, Mr. Hayden, yet, I think that underlying much of what you have said there is truth. Now, having squared off both extremes and gotten in trouble with each end, let me just ask you this: what specific institutional changes do you suggest we could make that would eliminate the necessity for, however you define it, your confrontation?

HAYDEN: I would say, Senator, that the problem there is not in the eyes of people who have grievances, but that there is not effective machinery. What are called channels turn out to be revolving doors at city hall or on a campus.

HART: I have got that clear enough. How do you fix it up?

HAYDEN: I am not sure that it can be fixed up from the top

because that would be a case of people on the top condemning themselves to less power. I think that is possible in our society, unlike other ones because we are so rich, that we would not have to fall into poverty. If you fell from the top, you would just write a check and some money would be redistributed and you would be the same person.

Specifically on the question of the draft, I think the most important thing that could be done would be to make it possible for individuals to have wider than religious objections to wars, that is, make conscientious objection a political category rather than a military one, which would have an underlying premise that the army apparently would not like, which is that the individual should choose what war he wants to fight.

I think that that is a most important right, to decide when you will pick up a gun and in whose country you will fight for what cause. That is with reference to the problem of how young people face the war, that is the point at which young people are forced into civil disobedience or disruption most often, because they cannot accept a draft system which they either dodge and feel morally uncomfortable by dodging; or in which they have to lie and say they are a Quaker or invent false descriptions of their religious beliefs; or they can be a conscientious objector in the army patching up people in the war that they don't want anybody to fight; or they can go into the war itself.

This is, I think, a most sacred right that everybody recognized, Daniel Webster and other people certainly recognized, long before—well, right down through our history until the Cold War and the establishment of the idea that you have to have a permanent military. With the idea there would be many wars in many places came the idea that people would not understand those wars, there might be objection to them, and in order to fight them you would have to have a permanent manpower pool that you could draw upon and regiment.

41

That interferes severely with the whole democratic process, I think. It would take a long time to answer your question further, but I could submit twenty or thirty similar proposals that you might call institutional changes which would not amount to a revolution on the one hand and would not amount to just a new gimmick which would not work and which would raise frustrations, but which would set up the possibilities for people to conduct their political differences more peacefully.

HART: My last question is perhaps a comment, although it might invite a reaction. In your comments to us you suggested that no longer was the New Left or SDS in the classic civil-disobedience category, that you suggested that you should not be punished when in your judgment some law was without moral support, as you define it. How can a society survive if it is up to the Ku Klux Klan to decide, or the SDS, and not have sanctions applied? Even if you came to power, how could you govern with that theory legitimately?

HAYDEN: The answer to that, that I have been trying to give, is you are putting the cart before the horse. The threat to the survival of the society comes from the illegal conduct of foreign policy and from the repeal—

HART: As some group decides it, as somebody decides it.

HAYDEN: As somebody decides it in a way which was an unrepresentative decision-making process and an undemocratic decision-making process. Once that has happened and the $100 billion is being spent for Vietnam, then these other questions come up, of what to do with people who feel that the channels are blocked and, therefore, they have to try to block the machinery in some way. At that point—

HART: If I could interrupt you so as to spare the time, perhaps we are in a chicken-and-egg fight. I am suggesting that I hear you indicate that anybody can make a determination with respect to the legitimacy of a society.

HAYDEN: Yes. That is as true for the right or the left wing.

HART: And that sanctions in your judgment should not be applied with respect to either of them because the other fellow, because a Klansman has as much right to claim that as you or I have.

HAYDEN: No. Sanctions will and should be applied to such behavior, but that raises again the question of who did the sanctioning and how did they get the power to do the sanctioning. If I respect the process by which they got the power, then I respect the sanction. That is the position of civil disobedience. Civil disobedience says I will break this law of yours but I respect your authority in general. So, I will break this law in order to bring its immorality to your attention. If you decide to punish me, I accept your right to punish me. If you decide that someone's authority now must be put into question because of the blind and insane way that he has used his authority, then you don't want to grant him the right to punish you for doing what you consider to be far more legitimate and moral than what he has done.

HART: If we were all saints, philosophers, scholars, and fortune tellers, we would all operate that way.

JAWORSKI: I seek a little more information on one matter. You make the statement, Mr. Hayden, that your group and in your group's work and your movement that violence has been almost nonexistent. Did I quote you correctly?

HAYDEN: Yes.

JAWORSKI: What do you mean by "almost," and in what places has it existed?

HAYDEN: You mean in student and antiwar and draft resistance?

JAWORSKI: In whatever sense you use it. You said in your group's movement—

HAYDEN: I just wanted to clear aside the question of the draft movement, because I am sure you are aware that some violence has occurred in that movement. There have been instances of what I would call retaliatory violence against police

43

and there have been instances of sabotage against private property. The sources of sabotage, of people who do it, I can't tell you because I don't know who they are, but I am not about to blame it on the right wing or the FBI which sometimes does things like this, but I will accept the likelihood that this is done by people who hate the war so much and hate the draft so much that they are willing to blow up private property that houses draft records, that houses chemical and biological and germ-warfare research and so forth.

The instances of this sabotage that I know of are from reading newspapers and hearing by word of mouth, the instances are miniscule. If you want what I mean numerically, I could probably guess that it is less than twenty-five instances in the last year. If you want the damage done in terms of dollars and cents, I couldn't tell you, but I am sure someone in the government could.

JAWORSKI: This is not in line with this policy, your movement, these acts of violence?

HAYDEN: No.

JAWORSKI: You don't approve of any of them yourself, do you?

HAYDEN: I will say this, I would not morally condemn a person who engages in such sabotage because I understand the way he feels. I think that a lot of people understand the way he feels. I think it is a counterproductive tactic. If he was involved in killing the poor secretaries who work in draft boards, then I would morally object and try to find ways to intervene. But so long as the damage is to private property, I would not morally condemn it while I do not think it is a useful tactic, although it has become fairly useful for the labor movement.

JAWORSKI: I am just interested in knowing now whether there is anything in your practices or policy that either espouses or condones such acts of violence that you have just described to us.

HAYDEN: The movement I am talking about is very loosely organized. There are several organizations, but none of them prescribes or supports—

JAWORSKI: Do you either espouse or condone those practices?

HAYDEN: I thought I answered that. I will not object to that practice of destruction of private property on moral grounds. I do not prescribe it or advocate it, and I know of no organization that does prescribe or advocate it.

JAWORSKI: You are in sympathy with it, that is what you are trying to say to us?

HAYDEN: I am in sympathy with senators who stand on the floor and denounce the war in Vietnam.

JAWORSKI: I am not talking about the war in Vietnam.

HAYDEN: I am in sympathy with anybody who is opposed to the war.

JAWORSKI: We are talking about destruction. These acts that you have described to us, are you in sympathy with them?

HAYDEN: Yes. I morally sympathize with people who feel that way. I don't think it is tactically or strategically effective.

JAWORSKI: That is all.

EISENHOWER: Menninger, may I warn you that the time is getting short.

MENNINGER: I must protest that. I feel it is very important, and with all due respect to the president of Yale University and all other people, I feel at this stage in time it might be very much more important for us to hear from this side of the situation than it is from the Establishment. Most of our hearings have been with the Establishment, and I do feel it is extremely important for us to have the time we need to be able to hear from this side of the story.

EISENHOWER: Let's don't discuss the commission's business here. We will discuss that at lunch.

MENNINGER: Let me say this: Mr. Hayden, one of the

things that perhaps concerns me more than anything else, if I am restricted to one question, has to do with the concept, if you will, of the self-fulfilling prophecy. You indicate in your opening statement that you had doubt in terms of coming here about the capacity to establish a dialogue and little hope for what might be accomplished. I think it is terribly important in our society to be able to establish that dialogue. I operate on a premise that I have expressed before, that sees in one sense violence as a breakdown in civilized communication, that when you cannot effectively communicate and carry on a dialogue, then you set up and begin to escalate.

My question has to do with this: Do you have awareness yourself of the activities, whether it is personal or of the organization, which you represent, that in effect contribute to the self-fulfilling hypothesis; namely, you begin with a strong view that the Establishment will not listen and then you operate in such a way as to demonstrate that the society or the Establishment will not listen. But you may or may not acknowledge the steps that you take that help bring about that solution.

HAYDEN: Are you suggesting that we never draw the conclusion that the Establishment will not listen?

MENNINGER: No.

HAYDEN: At what point in experience would you draw the conclusion?

MENNINGER: The point I am asking is: Do you subject yourself to the same scrutiny that you subject the Establishment to?

HAYDEN: Well, as you probably know, our movement talks within itself too much, probably, in my opinion, and not enough to others. It is one of the most healthily introspective protest movements that you could expect to find. I don't think that the problem is the problem of a self-fulfilling prophecy. I think if the shoe fits wear it.

If I call you something and you act that way merely because I called you that, then you should examine yourself and ask why you have acted in precisely the way that I predicted rather than blaming me for making you act in that way simply because I said you would.

JENNER: I don't share the observations of Dr. Menninger. I take it, Mr. Hayden, your view is that if he employs a method or means of communication, which is what we are really talking about, of a minority to a majority or of a majority to a minority, as the case might be, he is genuinely and is in his own mind morally convinced that his objective, morally or politically, is sound, that if he uses the method which even you, let us say—I will strike the wording—which you or which I would regard as excessive, if I may use a mild term, excessive to the point where some might describe it as violent, that he should be excused in the sense of not being called to respond to the rule of law, whatever rule of law may be applicable to that kind of conduct, the condemnation that society expresses in that rule or law, he should be excused; should he, is that your philosophy?

HAYDEN: You are describing the American way of life. That would be my answer to you. There are laws against the sale of poisoned meat. Several have been passed, one in 1905, another quite recently, where we brought poor old Mr. Upton Sinclair back and told him a new law was being passed to ban bad meat.

Second, there are laws regulating the conduct of merchants in the way that their scales are used, in the way that they advertise—Senator Hart knows far more than I do about the problems of advertising and packaging.

There are legal enforcement procedures for properly dealing with individuals who operate outside this framework. Yet, we know it is the way of life in the inner city for merchants to operate outside of this supposed rule of law and have the enforcement officers paid off or otherwise wink at their activities. So, the problem with respect for the law is an all-around question, a two-way street.

JENNER: Pardon the interruption. You are not answering my question.

HAYDEN: Well, it is not illegal in my opinion to steal from a merchant who is conducting himself that way. To arrest me for taking his property which is property which is organically illegal and which is used in illegal commerce is to put the cart before the horse, because I would certainly have no need to supposedly break the law if the law was originally respected.

JENNER: Mr. Chairman, I cannot obtain an answer to my question, and I yield.

HARRIS: This paper has been provocative, but in the interest of time, may I just limit myself to a comment, partly in line with what Senator Hart has said.

There are many things with which I agree and many things with which I disagree. To incorporate something that was suggested in Dr. Brewster's statement, I have a feeling that your assumption about the inability to secure dialogue with some part of the elite, the Establishment, the older generation, and all of the devils of your particular discussion are self-fulfilling prophecies which because of the very assumptions prevent the dialogue.

HIGGINBOTHAM: Mr. Hayden, I want to ask you one question because I am concerned as to whether there are any rather elementary mechanisms from which we as a country can move from protest to solution. Part of your thesis, as I understood it, was that youth has a feeling of impotence, and they cannot graft their sentiments into any type of significant action. Do you believe that reducing the voting age to eighteen would be a help in decreasing the frustration of the impotence?

HAYDEN: Yes, it would, if at the same time we had someone to vote for.

HIGGINBOTHAM: But you see no relationship between having the right to vote and having someone to vote for?

HAYDEN: No, not necessarily. You would increase frustrations of young people if they had a vote which had no effective means in the two-party system.

JENNER: The young people would then become the majority, would they not?

HAYDEN: We are getting there.

EISENHOWER: Right toward the end of your testimony you said, "The American system is impossible to reform. You must come around to our program."

I am very anxious and quite earnestly anxious to know what this program is that you would advocate if the present system cannot be reformed. So, if you have documents or would be prepared to submit one, I would appreciate it very much.

HAYDEN: I will try to do that with a brief statement now. I don't remember saying it exactly that way, and putting it that way slightly alters my meaning.

What I think I said was that the recent experience with electoral politics has convinced a large number of people that the electoral system is probably impossible to reform. Those were the exact words. You don't believe I said at all "come around to our program."

All that I can recall saying was I believe that in the future a majority of people who now are students and young people could be won to our program.

Part Two

HAYDEN: My full name is Thomas Emmett Hayden.

CONLEY: Mr. Hayden, would you give us a brief résumé of your educational background, please?

HAYDEN: Yes, I attended Royal Oak-Dondero High School in Royal Oak, Michigan, from 1954 to 1957. I attended the University of Michigan, 1957 to 1961. I returned to the University of Michigan 1962 through part of 1964, as a graduate student, and as an instructor, and I taught political science at Rutgers University in 1967.

CONLEY: I don't believe you mentioned it. Did you get a degree from the University of Michigan?

HAYDEN: I did not complete my graduate studies.

CONLEY: Did you get a bachelor's?

HAYDEN: I got a bachelor's degree in 1961.

CONLEY: Was this in English?

HAYDEN: Yes.

CONLEY: Now, Mr. Hayden, since your completion of your education, what particular positions have you held, since you completed your education?

HAYDEN: What do you mean by "positions"?

CONLEY: What jobs have you held, sir?

HAYDEN: You mean, jobs in the sense of how I get money?

CONLEY: Well, let us start with that, yes.

HAYDEN: Or political positions, or what?

CONLEY: Let us start with the jobs that you held where you get money.

HAYDEN: Well, I have done some teaching, as I said, at Rutgers University. I have been paid as an author and lecturer, published two books, one by New American Library–Signet, on North Vietnam, and another on the conditions in

53

Newark at the time of the rebellion of July, 1967, which was published by Random House.

CONLEY: Was this book *Rebellion in Newark?*

HAYDEN: Right. And I remain under contract, writing another book on Vietnam for the same publishing house.

CONLEY: All right. Now have you, in connection with your book writing, also written the preface to a book called *Mission to Hanoi?*

HAYDEN: You mean the book by Communist Party theoretician Herbert Aptheker.

CONLEY: Yes, sir.

HAYDEN: Yes, I traveled, I was a fellow traveler to Hanoi with Herbert Aptheker in 1965, and I did write an introduction to his book, before I proceeded to write a book giving my own political views.

CONLEY: Now then, these are the jobs that you have held where you received pay, as I understand.

HAYDEN: As far as I can recall.

CONLEY: Now, what jobs have you held in the political area, as you define it?

HAYDEN: Well, I consider myself an organizer of a movement to put you and your committee out of power, because I think you represent racist philosophy that has no meaning any more in the twentieth century.

CONLEY: What group do you refer to that you represent?

HAYDEN: I have worked for many groups. As you know, I worked very hard for several years for Students for a Democratic Society.

CONLEY: Were you president of that group from June of '62 to '63?

HAYDEN: I was president of SDS, yes, during the time that you designate. But before that, I was an organizer of it, and afterwards, I remained affiliated with it for some time.

CONLEY: Were you the author of the Port Huron Statement?

HAYDEN: I wish that I was, but I was merely a drafter of the original document, and the author of the document was the convention itself, that met in Port Huron.

CONLEY: You assisted, then, in the preparation of the document which was adopted by the convention?

HAYDEN: I was probably the major author of the original draft.

CONLEY: Was it materially changed by the convention?

HAYDEN: Yes. It had a better position on American capitalism. I was not too clear about the problems of American society and the convention straightened me out by deciding that the profit system that you represent is a fundamental thing to be moved aside, so that the country can move ahead.

CONLEY: Now, Mr. Hayden, a minute ago, in connection with your books, you mentioned that you had written a book about Vietnam. Was this book *The Other Side?*

HAYDEN: Right.

CONLEY: Did you collaborate on this book with the traveler that went with you, Mr. Lynd?

HAYDEN: Yes, I did.

CONLEY: And you coauthored this book together?

HAYDEN: Right.

CONLEY: And did I understand you correctly that this book came out subsequent to your preface to *Mission to Hanoi?*

HAYDEN: As far as I can recall, Herbert Aptheker's book came out rather quickly after the trip, and the book that I wrote with Staughton came out some time later.

CONLEY: Now, Mr. Hayden, moving to another area, and that is the National Mobilization Committee, were you the coproject director with Mr. [Rennie] Davis for the National Mobilization Committee's efforts in Chicago?

HAYDEN: Yes, I was.

CONLEY: When were you appointed to this position?

HAYDEN: I don't recall the exact date. I suppose it was in the early spring.

CONLEY: By whom were you appointed?

HAYDEN: By the Mobilization, which has a structure for making such appointments, consisting of an administrative committee, and a steering committee, and a set of officers.

CONLEY: Were you a part of the steering committee or the officers, or the—

HAYDEN: No.

CONLEY: How many people are represented by this group?

HAYDEN: The Mobilization has representatives from nearly a hundred organizations, most of whom are active around particular subjects like the organization of the demonstration.

CONLEY: Well, did 100 people meet to decide to appoint you?

HAYDEN: I can't really recall. If you will allow me one minute to go talk to Rennie Davis, who has more of an organizational mind than I do, I am sure I could straighten it all out, but the Mobilization, through its normal processes, appointed me in the spring of the year to be a project director with Rennie Davis, and I went to Chicago for that purpose.

CONLEY: Did you receive this appointment in writing, or was it just verbal?

HAYDEN: Oh, no, that's not the way we work.

CONLEY: Do you recall who actually told you that you had been appointed?

HAYDEN: No, I just knew that I had been appointed. I presume it was, if anyone told me that I was appointed, it was Dave Dellinger, who as you know is the chairman of the Mobilization.

CONLEY: Now, Mr. Hayden, when did you go to Chicago and begin working full time for the committee?

HAYDEN: I went to Chicago at the beginning of the summer. Again, the exact date is something I would have to check, but it was late May or early June.

CONLEY: And did you work out of the 407 South Dearborn Street address?

56

HAYDEN: Yes, I did.

CONLEY: Now at the time that you started to work for the committee, were you paid any type of a salary?

HAYDEN: No. I didn't take a salary. I lived from my normal income.

CONLEY: Did you, during any of the time that you worked with the National Mobilization Committee, receive any salary or compensation?

HAYDEN: Not that I know. I think they allocated some funds for the office staff, and those probably were in Rennie Davis' name. But I wasn't too close to that end of the organization, and my services were basically volunteer services.

CONLEY: Then, sir, is it your testimony that you received no compensation, either by check or by cash, for your activities in Chicago?

HAYDEN: As best as I can recall, I lived from my own income, but you see, the way we live, I mean, I give Rennie some money, and he might give it back to me, and in that sense, it may have gone through the Mobilization at one time or another, but basically, I always lived on my own income.

CONLEY: Well, sir, I can understand with cash that this might be true, but do you have any specific recollection of having received any checks in any way that were earmarked as monies for you as compensation for working with the National Mobilization Committee?

HAYDEN: There might have been some during the summer, but if there were, they were a pittance. Maybe $200.

CONLEY: You stated that you continued to live on your outside income. What was the source of your income?

HAYDEN: Speaking, based on the notoriety that people like you and the mass media have given me.

CONLEY: Your speaking appearances, then, were what you were able to derive your income from?

HAYDEN: And writing.

57

CONLEY: What particular articles were you writing at that time?

HAYDEN: Well, as I said, I was at work on a contractual basis with Random House on a new book on Vietnam.

CONLEY: Now, Mr. Hayden, Mr. Davis worked with you in the Chicago office, did he not?

HAYDEN: He primarily ran the office.

CONLEY: Did you consider him your boss?

HAYDEN: No. He was my brother.

CONLEY: How many other full-time employees did you have in the Chicago office?

HAYDEN: I don't know, because we don't operate on that basis. As the convention approached, we had more and more people working out of the office on a multitude of problems.

CONLEY: Starting in June, how many people did you have there in June?

HAYDEN: You see, because we have different views of the world, it sometimes may seem to you that I don't answer your questions, but that is primarily because I don't live in a world of jobs, money, and so forth.

CONLEY: No, sir, you have answered my question very nicely. I am just asking you—

HAYDEN: There is a number, I mean, I don't know how many people worked in the Chicago office in June. Probably ten or fifteen.

CONLEY: All right, sir, and then in July, do you have any statement as to how large the staff had grown to at that time?

HAYDEN: No.

CONLEY: A guesstimate?

HAYDEN: More.

CONLEY: More than—

HAYDEN: Twenty, twenty-five.

CONLEY: And then during the first two weeks of August, what had the staff grown to?

HAYDEN: I don't really know. It was larger, but see, it was

organized not in terms of numbers, but we were organizing a legal panel to handle our suit against Mayor Daley, seeking to get permits for our demonstrations and rallies, and I don't know if you would consider those lawyers part of the Mobilization staff.

We were organizing doctors, to prepare first-aid stations, because we expected that what with the announcement that 20,000 troops would be brought into the city, some people were going to get hurt, and we didn't want Mayor Daley's hospitals to be the only thing that we could go to if people were hit over the head, but I don't know if you would consider those doctors part of the Mobilization staff.

CONLEY: You considered them part of the Mobilization staff, didn't you?

HAYDEN: No, that is the doctors' group. We considered our responsibility was to make sure that sympathetic public-health students, medical students, and doctors would get themselves together and stay in touch with us about our programmatic needs, and the same with lawyers, so the question of staff involves a lot of blurred lines. That is all I am saying.

Out of the central office, Room 315, 407 South Dearborn, as I say, there was always a nucleus of ten to thirty people, doing the normal central office work, answering the phone, and sending out mailings, and protecting the doors from people who might want to come in and shoot the place up. That sort of thing occupied most of the people in the office, and as the convention approached, more and more people came to the office, at least to get some information about what was happening and where to go in the city. So it got to be a very large office situation, by the time of the convention.

CONLEY: Well, you, then, do I understand it that it is your testimony you did not consider the lawyers, then, and the doctors, who were part of the overall plan, as a part of the Mobilization committee?

59

HAYDEN: Well, we don't think in those terms.

CONLEY: Sir, you are the one that raised the question that I might think in those terms, and I am asking you what you thought?

HAYDEN: Yes, they didn't have to accept the Mobilization structure—I mean, they were not integral parts of it, in the sense of groups that would abide by all the day-to-day decisions or general policy decisions. They were more cooperating groups, cooperating groups of doctors and cooperating groups of lawyers.

CONLEY: All right, now after the convention was over, Mr. Hayden, did you then leave the Chicago area, and go to the West Coast?

HAYDEN: Yes.

CONLEY: And have you continued to remain on the West Coast, basically, since that time?

HAYDEN: Basically, since that time, yes.

CONLEY: And did you continue to receive in any way any compensation after the convention from the National Mobilization Committee?

HAYDEN: No.

CONLEY: Now, Mr. Hayden, did you remain in Chicago from the time you arrived there in June until the Democratic convention in August?

HAYDEN: Yes, I did, basically.

CONLEY: Did you leave there on at least one occasion, though, and go overseas?

HAYDEN: Yes, I went to Paris, to try to do some writing about the peace talks and to have discussions with Ambassador Harriman, and with North Vietnamese officials.

CONLEY: Now was this trip made in July of 1968?

HAYDEN: To the best of my recollection.

CONLEY: And did you meet, when you were in Paris, with the North Vietnamese, Viet Cong, and U.S. representatives, including Mr. Harriman?

HAYDEN: Yes, although I don't recall meeting with South Vietnamese representatives or Viet Cong, as you call them. I passed them briefly at a reception.

ASHBROOK: Mr. Counsel, he answered yes. You did meet with Mr. Harriman?

HAYDEN: Yes, of course.

CONLEY: Now when you had these contacts with the North Vietnamese in Paris, did you discuss with them a meeting between U.S. and Vietnamese youth to be held in Budapest, Hungary, in September of this year?

HAYDEN: No, I did not.

CONLEY: You had no discussion with them at all about that meeting in September?

HAYDEN: No.

CONLEY: Prior to making this trip, did you consult with Robert Greenblatt? Specifically with reference to this trip?

HAYDEN: No.

CONLEY: You had no discussion with Mr. Greenblatt, then, prior to making the trip to Paris?

HAYDEN: Of course I have had discussions with Mr. Greenblatt.

CONLEY: Sir, let me finish.

HAYDEN: —prior to the trip.

CONLEY: Sir, let me finish my question; I will try to let you finish your answer. You had no discussion with Mr. Greenblatt, specifically dealing with your making the trip to Paris, or what you were going to do in Paris?

HAYDEN: I probably did. It was not a very significant or important meeting, but since he was around the Mobilization office, he was aware that I would be going on my way to Paris, and to the best of my recollection, I probably did not speak to Greenblatt, because the trip to Paris was decided upon rather suddenly, and I didn't stop in New York on my way out. I am just trying to indicate that I may have talked to Greenblatt at some point before the trip, and if you would ask

61

something more specific, I might be able to answer more specifically.

CONLEY: All right, well, it is a fact, is it not, that Mr. Greenblatt and Dave Dellinger had been in Prague earlier, this summer, at a meeting with the Vietnamese representatives?

HAYDEN: Yes, I believe that is true.

CONLEY: All right, now had you had any discussion with them, with reference to this earlier meeting?

HAYDEN: What earlier meeting? Their meeting?

CONLEY: Their meeting in Prague.

HAYDEN: Not very extensive discussion, but I was aware that they had discussed in Prague a potential conference between Americans and Vietnamese, not unlike the conference that I had organized in Bratislava, Czechoslovakia, in September of 1967. But I was working on the Chicago project, and conferences with the Vietnamese in the fall were not particularly on my mind. That is all I am saying. My responsibility was to work on Chicago.

CONLEY: Would you say that you had made this trip to Paris as an emissary for David Dellinger, who had been in Europe earlier this summer? Were you responsible for transmitting any messages for Mr. Dellinger?

HAYDEN: It is not clear; are you referring again to the Budapest business, or what?

CONLEY: No, I am referring to your trip, sir. Your trip was to Paris.

HAYDEN: Well, not an emissary of David Dellinger. He is the chairman of the Mobilization, and I am a close associate of his, and, but I didn't—

CONLEY: Well, sir, I will use your word. Did you make your trip as a close associate of Mr. Dellinger—

HAYDEN: Of course.

CONLEY: —for the purpose of communication of messages from Mr. Dellinger to the group in Paris?

HAYDEN: Well, I think Mr. Dellinger was aware of what I

was doing, and we sort of think alike, so I wasn't communicating his message to Paris, so much as just communicating our own message.

CONLEY: Which would be both your messages, then, I take it, if you think alike.

HAYDEN: I think that is a safe conclusion.

CONLEY: Now, Mr. Vernon Grizzard has stated that he attended the Budapest meeting, and did you, before you leave for Paris, discuss with Grizzard, who was in charge of the marshals in Chicago, the possibility of his going to the Budapest meeting with the Viet Cong?

HAYDEN: Not that I recall, no.

CONLEY: You recall no conversations?

HAYDEN: I don't think that Vernon was ever definite about whether he was going to Budapest or not. I think that that was a rather late decision, but you would have to call him and ask him.

CONLEY: Now while you were in Paris, in July, did you have occasion to meet with Colonel Ha Van Lau?

HAYDEN: I met him briefly at a reception. I know Colonel Lau, from my trips to North Vietnam.

CONLEY: You had met with him previously, in '65 was it not?

HAYDEN: I was there December of '65, January, '66, and October, '67, and on those two occasions, I had extensive discussions with Ha Van Lau, because he is a very important spokesman, as you know, for the North Vietnamese. In addition to being a major member of their delegation in the Paris peace talks, he was a part of their delegation to Geneva in 1953–54. I believe that he was a member of the delegation in the 1962 conference to settle the Laotian situation.

He was the liaison between the North Vietnamese People's Armed Forces and the International Control Commission, which was set up by the Geneva Agreements. He was the Secretary-General of the North Vietnamese commission to in-

63

vestigate United States war crimes in Vietnam, and very instrumental in the tribunal that found the United States guilty of genocide.

CONLEY: What was his title in July of this year, when you met with him?

HAYDEN: He was probably still all of those things. I don't know. But he was basically functioning as a member of the North Vietnamese delegation. But don't misconstrue it. I didn't meet with him. I saw him by chance at a reception, and shook his hand, and didn't even exchange comments with him.

CONLEY: Do you recall who else you might have met with from the North Vietnamese delegation there in Paris?

HAYDEN: Yes. I met with Vietnamese, again, whom I had known from North Vietnam.

CONLEY: Yes, their names, sir.

HAYDEN: You want their names?

CONLEY: Yes, sir.

HAYDEN: Nguyen Minh Vy, and Xuan Oanh, which I am sure you racists will be able to pronounce. If you want the spelling, I can submit it.

CONLEY: Does this individual hold any official—

HAYDEN: That is two people.

CONLEY: I am sorry, sir. The first one. Let us go back to the first one.

HAYDEN: Well, they are members of the North Vietnamese delegation in Paris. It is currently involved in discussions with the United States government about ending the war. I don't know whether they have titles as such within the delegation.

CONLEY: Now did you also just meet these people at a reception?

HAYDEN: No, I had very extensive discussions with them, just as I did with Ambassador Harriman.

CONLEY: Now did you in your discussions with them discuss the forthcoming Democratic convention, and the National Mobilization Committee's role in the Chicago convention?

HAYDEN: I told them that what they were reading in the American papers was true, that we were involved very heavily in planning for that, but that wasn't the purpose of my visits with them.*

CONLEY: What was their reaction when you told them that?

HAYDEN: Well, they hoped very much that the American public would be able to make its desire known for the war in Vietnam to end, they hoped that public opinion would make itself felt on the government of the United States, and as you know, they certainly think that a peace movement is in the interests not only of the people of Vietnam, but the people of the United States.

So they are always very interested in demonstrations or activities in the United States against the war, although they believe that the reason there is a peace movement is because the United States has been defeated in Vietnam. They would never say that they could utilize public opinion in the United States, as some people apparently believe, to bring the war to an end. They believe the war will only be brought to an end in Vietnam itself, when the United States is stymied.

CONLEY: Were they pleased at the focusing that your committee was having on the people in the United States? Did they have any reaction to this, the methods being taken?

HAYDEN: They would never meddle in other people's affairs, contrary to your theories of aggression and infiltration, and so forth. They believe that the people—

CONLEY: Sir, I am not interested in what—

* HUAC tried to imply that the basic reason for the Paris trip was to consult the Vietnamese about the Chicago demonstration. This would indicate their theory that the peace movement is directed from Hanoi. However, the basic reason for my trip was to make technical arrangements for the release of three captured U.S. pilots from North Vietnam. During the HUAC hearings I continually attempted to lure them into asking more about Paris, but they avoided the subject when they realized I was willing to discuss it.

HAYDEN: People who have a problem—

CONLEY: Just a minute, now. My question requires a yes or no answer.

HAYDEN: I am—

CONLEY: My question requires a yes or a no, and then you can give your explanation.

HAYDEN: I will give better than a yes or no. I mean, I am not going to equivocate before this Committee.

ICHORD: Let the witness proceed. We are going along very well here.

HAYDEN: If you want to state your question again, I will go at it more bluntly, or I will reduce it and make it simpler for you.

CONLEY: Was the North Vietnamese delegation pleased or did they have any reaction to the fact that your National Mobilization Committee was serving as a focal point for bringing this issue to the attention of the American people, through the Democratic convention?

HAYDEN: Well, they are pleased at any kind of peace activity or any sign that people are beginning to come to their senses about Vietnam, so of course they are pleased about whatever the antiwar movement is trying to do in the United States: including demonstrations at the convention, including resistance to the draft, including traveling and speaking around the country on college campuses. Whatever we do for peace in Vietnam, that we think is in our interest, is obviously in their interest, because they want peace in Vietnam.

CONLEY: Mr. Hayden, moving to another area, and taking you back, if I may, to about February of this year, back to February 11, 1968, actually, this is apparently when the first meeting of the National Mobilization Committee in relation to the Democratic convention in Chicago was held; apparently this meeting was cochaired by Rennie Davis and Carlos Russell.

66

HAYDEN: What was the date of that, again?

CONLEY: February 11, 1968?

HAYDEN: In Chicago?

CONLEY: Yes. It was held in Chicago, on February 11, 1968.

HAYDEN: At 407 South Dearborn?

CONLEY: Sir, I don't know the address.

HAYDEN: Is that the meeting that I think this fellow here—

CONLEY: If you will let me complete the question, I think you will know what meeting I mean. The meeting was co-chaired by Rennie Davis and Carlos Russell, and established an interim committee composed of yourself, Rennie Davis, Dave Dellinger, Robert Greenblatt, Earl Durham, Corky Gonzales, Carolyn Black, Lincoln Lynch, Sue Munaker, which was for the purpose of continuing the organization and planning of the project in Chicago.

Now my question, sir, is did you attend that meeting?

HAYDEN: Yes, I did.

CONLEY: And the address is 407 South Dearborn?

HAYDEN: Yes, sir.

CONLEY: Now do you recall who invited you to take part in that meeting?

HAYDEN: No.

CONLEY: Whether it was by a verbal invitation, by written notification? You do not recall?

HAYDEN: Well, I wanted the meeting to happen, and just assumed that I would be there. I was among the people who probably organized for the meeting, although I wasn't living in Chicago at the time.

CONLEY: Now, Mr. Hayden, was it prior to, or subsequent to, this meeting that you and Rennie Davis coauthored the document, "Movement Campaign 1968—An Election Year Offensive," which was dated March, 1968, and marked "Not for Publication"?

HAYDEN: I think that it was after. I think that we sort of

took into account a lot of opinions expressed at that meeting, and then we wrote the document. To the best of my recollection, that is what I will testify to now.

CONLEY: Now, did you and Rennie Davis also prepare another document for the National Mobilization Committee, entitled "Discussion on the Democratic Convention Challenge," and this document likewise was marked "Not for Publication," but was addressed to the Chicago organizers?

HAYDEN: I don't know. I don't remember such a document. If you will show it to me, I can easily tell you who wrote it.

(The document was handed to the witness.)

HAYDEN: Is this—this is it?

CONLEY: Yes, sir.

HAYDEN: Yes, of course we authored it. It says we did. I just didn't remember the title. See, it is not really a title. It just says discussion on the Democratic convention challenge. I think that was kind of a warmup for the later paper.

CONLEY: All right, now do you recall when this particular document was prepared?

HAYDEN: Oh, yes, it was—it was prepared sometime between January and February.

CONLEY: Now I believe this document is marked "To the Chicago organizers." Who were the Chicago organizers to whom this document was directed?

HAYDEN: Well, I don't think it was directed to Chicago organizers any more than anybody else, so I don't know. You see, I didn't type this, and I don't know what that particularly refers to, but it probably, when the term "Chicago organizers" is used, that probably means that this document was circulated among active people throughout the city, who organize tenant unions, organize rent strikes against slum landlords, organize black people in the ghetto, organize draft resisters, organize students on campuses; you know, organizers.

Rennie was a Chicago organizer, as you know, for some

68

time, working with poorer working-class white people on the North Side of Chicago, and he probably means by this that this memorandum was sent out to other organizers around the city.

That is a very revealing document, in terms of what our intentions were. I hope that it is in your record, because it indicates that our intention was never to disrupt the convention or engage in violence. And I hope that also part of the record is the fact that we had a vote, according to this document that you gave me, on what kind of demonstration we wanted to have. This was at this February meeting you are referring to, when we voted against the view of disruption, which you have marked here, or someone has marked here, where it says, "One view holds that the movement shall prevent the convention from assembly. The movement should do everything possible to disrupt its deliberations in August," and as part of the record, we voted against that view, in favor of another view.

CONLEY: Now, Mr. Hayden, going back to the meeting of February 11, you have stated that you were present at that meeting that occurred.

HAYDEN: I must have been.

CONLEY: Did you hear Communist party official Donald Hammerquist say, and I quote as follows:

"What we must do is make concrete demands on the convention which the convention can't respond to."

HAYDEN: Well, that would be a typical communist party position, based on the idea that you have to organize people where they are at, and realize that you authorities will never give them even the smallest reward, so it wouldn't surprise me if Hammerquist said that.

CONLEY: Did you recall him saying that, sir?

HAYDEN: No, I don't recall it. But it wouldn't surprise me in the least.

CONLEY: All right.

HAYDEN: By that he would mean, if you organize to demand housing for everybody in America, they will find out that you people never give housing to everybody in America.

CONLEY: All right, and then, Mr. Hayden, were you present when Communist party member Jack Spiegel stated, "We can't call to"—

HAYDEN: By the way, I don't know if any of these people are members of the Communist party. This is your committee, and your tape recorders, and you can go right ahead, but it is not my designation.

CONLEY: Well, sir, I hand you back the convention notes.

HAYDEN: Jack Spiegel is designated as a Communist party member?

CONLEY: I don't know what "C. P." stands for, sir.

HAYDEN: Chicago Peace Council, Jack Spiegel.

CONLEY: Look at Hammerquist, please.

HAYDEN: You didn't ask me about Hammerquist. When you said "Communist party member Jack Spiegel" I interrupted you; when you said "Communist party member Hammerquist" I didn't interrupt, because everybody knows he is a member of the Communist party. It is listed.

CONLEY: All right. Moving on to Mr. Spiegel.

ASHBROOK: Mr. Counsel, is it listed on that book?

HAYDEN: It just says, "C. P." I assume that means "Communist party." But Jack Spiegel is listed as Chicago Peace Council.

CONLEY: All right, Mr. Spiegel's quote as follows: "We can't"—

HAYDEN: What are you reading from? Some stolen notes, or what?

CONLEY: From your February 11, page 4, column two.

HAYDEN: Just give me the page, and you won't have to read it. Okay, what is it?

CONLEY: All right, the quote is, "We can't call 200,000 people to Chicago and then disassociate ourselves from violence. Disruption and violence will occur. It is going to happen, and we will have to deal with that fact."

Now, were you present when this statement was made by Mr. Spiegel?

HAYDEN: Well, you haven't read it, of course. But I was present during the meeting. I don't remember him saying it, but if you will read the whole statement, I think you will find it is very interesting. Mr. Spiegel does not mean that—

CONLEY: Now, sir, I am not interested in what—

HAYDEN: Just a minute—

CONLEY: That isn't responsive to my question, sir.

HAYDEN: I was present, but I think it is fair for you to read all of Mr. Spiegel's statement, and I will read it for you, if you won't read it.

CONLEY: I am just asking you if Mr. Spiegel made this statement.

HAYDEN: Then I have to say I don't know, but I will go further and say that you haven't read his entire statement.

CONLEY: I am asking you, sir, though, did he make this statement?

HAYDEN: You had better call him and ask him.

CONLEY: I am asking you if you heard him make that statement.

HAYDEN: I can't remember him saying it, but here it is in the notes, so I assume he said something like that. What is the big deal that you are uncovering by reading from a note? I mean obviously he said something like that, or it wouldn't be in the notes, but the main problem is you haven't read his entire statement, which tries to point out that we are going to have to organize an alternative to violence.

ICHORD: The entire statement is a matter of record, is it not, Mr. Counsel?

CONLEY: Yes, sir.

HAYDEN: Not for the press in this room, who are listening to your slander of Mr. Spiegel.

CONLEY: It has been previously introduced as Exhibit 4 at the earlier hearings.

❊   ❊   ❊

CONLEY: Mr. Hayden, directing your attention to page 4, column one, of your convention notes, the document prepared as a result of the February eleventh meeting? There appears there a statement which apparently is attributed to you, beginning at the top of the page, "As organization develops to challenge the Democratic Party, it must project a nonviolent, legal face. We can't call for violence, although violence is a major method of change in this society."

Did you make this statement, sir?

HAYDEN: I made a statement to that effect. But again, you haven't read my entire statement, which is typical of a witch hunt.

ICHORD: You wish the entire statement read?

HAYDEN: Either that, or if you would let me tell you why I think violence is a major tool of change, I would be glad to do that.

ICHORD: I think the question permits such an answer. Go ahead.

HAYDEN: Fine.

I believe that violence should never be ruled out as a method of change, especially, I believe that a country that is burning up Vietnam has no right to lecture people to be nonviolent. However, I believe also, I always believed, that Chicago was no place for a violent confrontation, because you have a disciplined, armed force of 20,000 men waiting for you there, and you have unarmed demonstrators straggling in, nineteen- and twenty-year-old kids from all around the country, who don't know each other, and they would be wiped out. They almost were wiped out in Chicago, simply for existing.

So I wanted to make a distinction in that meeting between the fact that I believe that at some point there may be increased violence in American society on the one hand and/or on the other hand I didn't believe that violence should be part of the planning or preparation or conception of Chicago.

I thought that what we were doing in Chicago was trying to sort of bring the kind of people who are the rank and file of the Democratic party, decent, middle-class Americans of all ages and classes and races, who believe in peace and social justice, to come and protest the abandoning of those ideals by the government of the United States.

And I know very well that for that kind of purpose, violence or the threat of violence only scares people away, and that is what I think Mayor Daley and President Johnson were engaged in by their buildup, military buildup; they were trying to scare people away from coming to the convention.

So I make no secret of the fact that I am not nonviolent, but often people who are not nonviolent can be the most nonviolent, because they know what they are doing, and they want to make sure that the means suit the ends, and the means in this case for me was a mass mobilization of a peaceful kind. It became a violent situation because of the Chicago Police Department, of which this committee is, I believe, an extension.*

ASHBROOK: I think your statement regarding your preference that there might be a confrontation at that time would certainly be borne out by what you have said in the past, but isn't it also true that you probably, on the basis of your other statements, would prefer urban guerrilla type of activity rather than a direct confrontation with 20,000 policemen?

* All HUAC's "friendly" witnesses who preceded us to the stand were members of the Chicago police department.

I note from your interview in the *National Guardian* on July 1, 1967, page 4, where you say, "Urban guerrillas are the only realistic alternative at this time to electoral politics and mass armed resistance."

HAYDEN: I am glad you brought that up. I have been meaning to settle that score with the *National Guardian* for some time. What I said was that we have to function as political guerrillas. I didn't say "urban guerrillas."

A political guerrilla is a person who uses the political concepts of guerrilla warfare without the weapons or the guns. The political concept of guerrilla warfare is to make yourself at one with the people you are trying to organize, be among them, go through their day-to-day existence, live on the same budget as they do, and organize them into a political force.

ASHBROOK: Sort of American Viet Cong?

HAYDEN: It would not be an American Viet Cong, until the day we started taking your guns from your police stations and turning them on you, and as far as I know, that hasn't happened, so you are making an extremely mistaken generalization that is merely meant to kind of paint the antiwar movement, the movement which is for peace in Vietnam, as somehow being an aggressive, violent movement. It is a case of the criminal calling the victim the criminal.

ASHBROOK: It is your position, when you said "urban guerrillas," you were not referring to urban guerrillas in the general context that most of us would think of urban guerrillas?

HAYDEN: I gave a speech saying that I believed that parliamentary means would be blocked in this society as we saw at the convention, the parliamentary efforts of Senators McGovern and McCarthy were blocked, and I felt that violent revolution was also not possible in the kind of society that we had, that therefore we had to find some kind of alternative to the traditional concepts of social change, which on the one hand is to overthrow the government, and on the other hand is to elect yourself president.

74

We have to find another way and the way that I think is to organize a movement of people who are very strong-minded and organized on local levels around their own grievances, and are able to win more and more people to their side, against the landlords and the tax collectors, and the generals and the draft boards who are raping them.

ASHBROOK: Maybe I didn't make my question clear, but specifically, when you, or at least when the reference attributed to you to urban guerrillas was used, you were not referring to the RAM-type of urban guerrilla, snipers, and so forth?

HAYDEN: Oh, no, I was not referring to warfare in a military sense, and it was a misquote that I am sorry about, and have always had some problems of interpretation because of that statement.

WATSON: Mr. Chairman, since we have interrupted the continuity of Counsel's questions, did I understand you earlier to say that you make no secret of the fact that you are nonviolent?

HAYDEN: I am not nonviolent, is what I said.

WATSON: You are not nonviolent. Now am I to construe, then, you believe in violence?

HAYDEN: No more than you do. Probably less than you do.

WATSON: Is that right? Now one further—

HAYDEN: Especially given your political background in South Carolina, I believe that to be the case.

WATSON: Well, fortunately, I believe the gentleman is not as well read about South Carolina activities as he may be about some others, because we have been—

HAYDEN: I just read about all that disenfranchisement.

WATSON: —relatively free of that down there. Of course, we could debate that back and forth, and you are far less knowledgeable than others around you, and you, when you stated earlier that you did not advocate violence in Chicago, your position was based upon the fact that there was an overwhelming force of some 20,000 policemen who would annihilate you, virtually, that's what you said?

HAYDEN: No, my basic reason was that I really wanted all along for the largest possible number of people to come, and that includes people with families, people bringing babies, and they would have to be guaranteed some safety, coming to Chicago.

They are afraid of Chicago because of what they have heard about Chicago, and so we fought, throughout the spring and summer, with Chicago officials to try to get permits so that this number of people could come into Chicago safe and sound, and go out, and my own interpretation of why the city refused us permits is because they didn't want all those people to come, and they knew perfectly well that the average person, like yourself, with family, would not go somewhere if he is afraid that he might be locked up, or get hit over the head, because people can't take those kind of chances. There were babies, even so, in Grant Park when the tear gas came. Tear gas can kill a baby.

WATSON: In other words, your position is that we have these things without the provocation by such groups as you represent?

HAYDEN: I didn't understand that.

WATSON: In other words, your position is that we have such brutality as you alleged without the provocations by such groups as you represent?

HAYDEN: Well, there is no question that we are a provocation to you. But why? It is only because we exist. Since when is obscenity, for example, a reason for a policeman to hit you over the head?

WATSON: In other words, you as an individual would welcome anyone to use any obscene language, in cursing you, or anything else, and you would just stand back quietly and fold your hands, and say, "Thank you"?

HAYDEN: If I was a public servant, engaged in protecting the law and order, I would not see obscenity as a threat to law and order.

WATSON: Oh, in other words, now we put you and the other citizens in a different category from a public official? A public official, in your estimation, is to take all types of abuse, whereas you or I or others, who are not public officials, they are to be so restrained, and so on. Is that your position? I guess basically it is.

HAYDEN: What do we pay taxes to our government for if it is not to have a professional government that is capable of having a police force to—

WATSON: —to suffer all types of abuse and profanity and obscenity and so forth? That is your basic position, isn't it? You enjoy a safe position, whereas the policeman, by virtue of his office, should expect abuse and all of that from organizations and individuals such as you?

HAYDEN: Well, I pity the policemen, frankly.

WATSON: I certainly do, when confronted with individuals like you.

HAYDEN: You haven't asked me enough about what I think to draw your conclusions.

WATSON: Let's reduce it to its simplest common denominator.

HAYDEN: What is that, Mr. Watson?

WATSON: You expect the policeman to accept, by virtue of his position, all types of abuse against him, whereas you as an individual would not accept such abuse, without retaliation?

HAYDEN: Why don't you ask me why policemen are sworn at sometimes? I mean, you don't just get mad at a person like this fellow here.* I have nothing obscene to say to him, because he is not doing anything to me. His uniform doesn't

* "This fellow here" is a reference to the police officer guarding the hearing who seemed to be interested in the arguments.

77

disturb me any more than your suit disturbs me. Even the fact that he has a gun doesn't disturb me, if he has a gun. He hasn't done anything. I am not being obscene to him.

Now why do you think somebody suddenly screams profanity at a policeman? Why do you think he does it? I would say it is because he has seen the policeman charge into a crowd, and beat somebody. And especially when it is at the order of Mayor Daley. I mean, a lot of abuse has been heaped on the Chicago police, and it is not really their fault. They were obeying the orders of Mayor Daley and people higher up, because when we went to jail, they didn't beat us in jail, they didn't act like irrational monsters in jail.

But what they did on the streets, they did in a highly disciplined way. They charged into crowds, they hit people in a disciplined way, they were carrying out orders, and when people are doing that to you, then you—at the very least—have a right to think obscene thoughts about their behavior—especially if Mayor Daley can say on television what he said to Abraham Ribicoff, which goes far beyond anything said to a policeman, as you will find out, when it is revealed next week. He made an anti-Semitic remark; he used all the language to Ribicoff that he accused us of using.* He is still the mayor of Chicago. He has not been called before you. He is not going to jail like we probably are. So let's not put the cart before the horse, Mr. Watson.

WATSON: Now, getting back to the basic question I asked you, the policeman, in your judgment—

HAYDEN: We have handled that question.

WATSON: The policeman, in your judgment, is expected by virtue of his position to accept all of the verbal abuse, but you as an individual are not expected—

* Senator Ribicoff's campaign staff asked a lip-reader at a school for the deaf to look at the television films of the scene. The official translation, as reported to Ribicoff: "Fuck you you Jew son of a bitch you lousy motherfucker go home."

HAYDEN: Verbal abuse does not come out of thin air. Verbal abuse comes from an initial abuse, an abuse on the part of a police officer, which is very evident, which is evident in this enormous report, which I would like to introduce into the evidence.* I have it here, it has 1,400 witnesses to police brutality in the city of Chicago. It is not going to be printed by any other government agency, and so my lawyers plan to introduce it today, so that at least some government agency will publish it with all of its obscene words and all the rest of it, and you can see for yourself who transgressed first.

WATSON: One final question—

HAYDEN: The other major thing I want to say in answer to your question is simply again that I believe that even if someone verbally abuses a police officer, a good, solid professional police officer has no reason to act as jury, judge, and executioner towards the person who used profane language against him.

WATSON: In other words, he is to stand there and accept it, quietly fold his hands, even—

HAYDEN: If a person has violated the law, the duty of the police officer is to arrest the person, not to engage in profanity with the person, not to engage in brutality with the person, but simply to carry out the law, and these policemen know that.

WATSON: May I ask you one final question, then—

HAYDEN: It is an insult to police to think that they somehow are incapable of controlling themselves when abused. I think they are capable of it. I think that they were ordered into action by Mayor Daley. It was not the taunts of the demonstrators, it was not these bags of urine, it was nothing like that; it was the fact that they were ordered by Mayor Daley

---

* On the morning of my testimony, the National Commission on Violence issued without comment the Walker Report, which called Chicago a "police riot." The less-sophisticated HUAC was clearly embarrassed by the document.

79

to get these yippies out of the streets, because a person like Mayor Daley does not believe that we have a right to exist.

That's our crime, that we exist; we have long hair, we smoke dope, we are opposed to the war in Vietnam, and so we shouldn't exist.

WATSON: So the preparation of the bags of urine and other things, they were just in the normal routine?

HAYDEN: I didn't see the bags of urine. I meant these supposed bags of urine.

WATSON: Let me ask you one other thing. You say you have 1,400 affidavits there?

HAYDEN: Let's see the *New York Times,* and I will tell you. It is the whole report which I am interested in.

WATSON: How many demonstrators do you estimate that you had out there?

HAYDEN: The police figure for Grant Park on August 28 was 15,000. That was the largest official figure or journalistic figure given, and everybody agrees that—

WATSON: So you had a minimum of at least 15,000 demonstrators?

HAYDEN: Oh, no. The police said fifteen. Everybody agreed that that was the largest number, August 28. That was the largest number for that peaceful rally in Grant Park. Before that, I think it was far less. We were outnumbered by the forces of law and order, so to speak, by about five to one, I would say.

WATSON: I see. If it had been equal, perhaps you really would have made a challenge at that time?

HAYDEN: Hardly. Hardly.

WATSON: One final thing—

HAYDEN: Unless you think that in man-to-man combat without weapons I can somehow handle this officer here. I don't think I can.

WATSON: But you have some 1,400 or 1,600 affidavits?

HAYDEN: Not affidavits, just—

WATSON: Statements.

HAYDEN: There is a report that has been published that consists of testimony taken by an authorized task force of the National Commission to Seek Inquiry into the Causes of Violence, and I think they have something like 1,400 witnesses.

ICHORD: Are these statements under oath, Mr. Hayden?

HAYDEN: I don't know. Why don't you call these witnesses in? They will tell you about police brutality under oath.

WATSON: Were they affidavits?

HAYDEN: I simply want to introduce it to you. Are you saying that this other government commission's study is invalid?

WATSON: I am simply asking, are these affidavits, or are they just statements?

HAYDEN: It is the report of the commission, which is an authorized government task force, which made the preposterous number of interviews to come to the conclusion that anyone could come to by watching television.

WATSON: But you never intended to cause violence at all?

HAYDEN: Absolutely not.

WATSON: Absolutely not; so all of the preparation, the training in the park—

HAYDEN: What preparation, Mr. Watson?

WATSON: Well, I assumed that you had to make a little preparation.

HAYDEN: What preparations?

WATSON: Having these bags of urine, and the sticks and the razor blades and the stones and the nails in the golf balls, and so forth.

HAYDEN: That is quite a joke.

WATSON: In other words, your position is you deny that any of these things were there or used by the demonstrators?

HAYDEN: No, I do not deny that.

WATSON: Thank you. That's all.

81

HAYDEN: But I deny that preparations were made.

WATSON: Do you allege that these things were used by the police, then?

HAYDEN: You mean the tear gas and the Mace?

WATSON: Oh, no, the bags of urine and golf balls.

HAYDEN: Would you rather be hit by a bag of urine or by Mace? Let's get first things first. Even if there were bags of urine, and I didn't see any, Mr. Watson—I didn't see any—I would still rather be hit by a bag of urine than be hit by Mace. That may be because you have never been hit by Mace, you have never been hit by your own cattle prods in South Carolina.

WATSON: Frankly, I have never been hit by either, and I would not venture to say what I might do if hit by either, but I will assure you of one thing—

HAYDEN: What would you do?

WATSON: I would not sit by and quietly fold my hands and do nothing; I—

HAYDEN: You would break the law?

WATSON: —I will assure you of that.

HAYDEN: You would throw a bag of urine? What would you do?

WATSON: Well, I can assure you of one thing, that I would not sit back quietly and do nothing if that were done to me.

HAYDEN: Would you swear? Would you swear at the person who did it to you? Or do you only do that at home?

WATSON: Whatever would meet your satisfaction. If that statement needs to be sworn, I will swear to that.

HAYDEN: Look, this is your hearing, not mine. I am not really interrogating you.

ICHORD: Gentlemen.

HAYDEN: I would like to redirect the question back to Paris, though, because I think incomplete testimony was given there, and you tried to imply something about the meetings in Paris that I want to correct, and go back there, and tell you what really was being done in Paris. So at some point, when you find it feasible, let's go back to that, so that the record will be absolutely clear.

ICHORD: We can get into that later on.

CONLEY: I think we will get back to Paris. Let's go back to February 11, 1968. The first meeting that was held in the National Mobilization Committee to organize for Chicago. Mr. Hayden, were you aware at the time of your attendance at that meeting that the following persons were in attendance at that meeting who were identified as members of the Communist party?

HAYDEN: Identified by whom?

CONLEY: By this committee, sir.

HAYDEN: I don't pay any attention to your committee.

CONLEY: All right. Well—

HAYDEN: I mean, you identify almost everybody in the United States as a member of the Communist party.

CONLEY: Kendra Alexander?

HAYDEN: Now what is the question? Was I aware she was there?

CONLEY: Yes.

HAYDEN: Or was I aware that she was identified by your committee as a communist, or what?

CONLEY: My question was: Were you aware that she was there and identified as a member of the Communist party?

HAYDEN: No.

CONLEY: You were not aware that she was there then?

HAYDEN: Yes, I was aware she was there.

CONLEY: Thank you, sir. Earl Durham?

HAYDEN: I was aware he was there.

CONLEY: Thank you, sir.

HAYDEN: You have these names underlined. What is that for?

CONLEY: Don Hammerquist?

HAYDEN: Yes, he was there.

CONLEY: Charlene Mitchell?

HAYDEN: She was there.

CONLEY: Jack Spiegel?

HAYDEN: And he was there. I mean, I don't exactly remember, but I assume they were there.

CONLEY: All right. Were you aware that Charlene Mitchell, mentioned previously, was the presidential candidate for the Communist party, U.S.A., during the 1968 campaign?

HAYDEN: That came as an interesting and pleasant surprise later. I think it is good that a black woman runs for president of the United States. I think it is good that Communists are back entering American politics, even though I don't agree with their political program. But I doubt that even she knew that she would be a candidate for president of the United States at the time, and that was the first time that I had met her, and I probably didn't even know her name.

CONLEY: Now if I may, again, you said that you did not know that Kendra Alexander had been identified as a member of the Communist party?

HAYDEN: I don't pay any attention to who you identify. If I had to read all your reports—

CONLEY: Earl Durham?

HAYDEN: Earl Durham what? Was I aware that he had been identified by you? No.

CONLEY: Don Hammerquist?

HAYDEN: Same question?

CONLEY: Well, you can look at your own document, though.

HAYDEN: Is he identified by your group as a member of the Communist party?

CONLEY: I will restate the question to Mr. Hayden.

HAYDEN: What is it you want to know? Everyone knows that there are—

ICHORD: The reporter is having difficulty following the interchange there. It is very fast. Let's ask the question again.

84

CONLEY: Let's go back and pick up the last question, and then move forward. Were you aware, from examining your own document, that Don Hammerquist was identified by your group as a member of the Communist party?

HAYDEN: You know, the Communist party and anybody else opposed to the war in Vietnam can participate in the Mobilization, so what? I mean, I don't understand why you are continuing the tradition of trying to point at these individuals if you have pointed at them before. I would be only too happy to discuss a general question, but I don't understand what you are saying.

CONLEY: As I understand your answer to an earlier question, Charlene Mitchell's candidacy for president on the Communist party was not known to you at that time?

HAYDEN: No. I didn't know anything about her.

CONLEY: You learned that sometime later?

HAYDEN: I learned from the papers.

CONLEY: Do you recall when, approximately, you learned that?

HAYDEN: When it was announced in the papers.

CONLEY: Do you have any estimate as to when that was, sir?

HAYDEN: No. I am sure you do.

CONLEY: Mr. Hayden, these ones that are not identified by your document, which are identified by this committee, do you have any knowledge, yourself, that they are members of the Communist party?

HAYDEN: No, I don't. Except, of course, Mrs. Mitchell, from what I read in the papers.

CONLEY: Now, Mr. Hayden, referring back to your document, "Movement Campaign 1968—An Election Year Offensive"—did you describe this document as follows: "This paper proposes an election year campaign against a political system that has brought the United States into a crisis of war, racism, and social disintegration. We outline a possible strategy for this campaign"?

HAYDEN: I notice that your hand is shaking as you read those stated purposes.

ICHORD: That is not being responsive to the question, Mr. Hayden.

HAYDEN: I think Rennie wrote that. It is on the first page. It is kind of a description of what is inside. This is just a little taste of what is to come, you know. It is just a cover.

CONLEY: Now, Mr. Hayden, moving to page 15 of that document, did you make the following statements on that page, "Black rebellions. In our view, summer organizers working in the white community should discuss plans in each training school for support and parallel activity during black ghetto rebellions"?

HAYDEN: I wrote that.

CONLEY: "Whites should sit in at Democratic mayors' offices"?

HAYDEN: I wrote that.

CONLEY: "Organize medical and legal support"?

HAYDEN: Yes.

CONLEY: "Pull together diversionary demonstrations outside the ghetto"?

HAYDEN: Yes, that even happened.

CONLEY: "To draw off police and find ways to focus public blame for what happened on the powerful white interests"?

HAYDEN: Yes, you should talk to Rennie about this also, because he did just that with a lot of white people in Chicago in April. He organized demonstrations against the presence of the National Guard in the city, with a lot of other Chicago groups, and those people were bayoneted, for carrying flowers, I believe, and gassed.

CONLEY: Now, getting back to this particular statement, is what you meant by that statement that whenever a race riot broke out in a ghetto area, that you were desirous that the

86

white community engage in simultaneous violent action in other parts of the community? Is this what you meant?

HAYDEN: No, you see, it is because you don't understand revolution. You can't start a revolution in your little suburb or on your campus just because the blacks over here started one. You don't do something because of something that is happening somewhere else. You don't try to do the same thing.

What this means is, we felt that white people who are sympathetic on these questions have been sort of paralyzed by the situation in which there were these ghetto rebellions, the police could come in, and like in Newark, they killed twenty-four black people in five days, wounded hundreds, put a couple of thousand in jail, and sympathetic whites could find no way to react, except by feeling paralyzed, watching television, and so on, and we thought that this had to end, and we had to show that not all white people favored the brutal suppression of justified rebellion, and so we wanted white people to conduct demonstrations in the suburbs and at the police stations and at the mayors' offices and, if necessary, place ourselves nonviolently in front of the National Guardsmen.

CONLEY: Simultaneously?

HAYDEN: Sure, at the time that it is happening. Like in Boston.

CONLEY: And in the same community?

HAYDEN: No, not necessarily. In Boston this spring there was the threat of an outbreak in the ghetto. It started one night, and the next day a local group there organized a big rally of white people against bringing in troops to suppress those people, and 20,000 white people came, and there were speeches, and I think that had a small political effect in sort of cooling the situation, and keeping the troops out.

CONLEY: Well, Mr. Hayden, in your statement, you say to pull together diversionary demonstrations outside the ghettos to draw off police. My question was: did you mean in the same community? You are not suggesting, sir, that if there were a black rebellion in Newark, New Jersey, that a white demonstration in Los Angeles would pull off any police, are you?

HAYDEN: That would be very good, even though it wouldn't pull off Newark police. I think a better place would be to go have a big demonstration at the temple where the landlords go to worship and another big demonstration at the Roman Catholic church, where the police go to worship, and raise questions about what they are doing in uniform, carrying the machine guns and automatic weapons down into the ghetto.

CONLEY: In Los Angeles or in Newark?

HAYDEN: No, right in the suburbs outside of Newark.

CONLEY: That's what I am trying to get at, sir. That's what we have been trying to get at, sir.

HAYDEN: Do you get it?

CONLEY: I think we are getting it.

HAYDEN: Okay.

CONLEY: Are all landlords Jewish?

HAYDEN: No.

CONLEY: I misunderstood your statement.

HAYDEN: But that's where most landlords tend to go, and most policemen tend to go to Roman Catholic Church, and that's where their conscience is, and that's where we should try to raise the question of how far they have strayed from their conscience. I certainly meant no ethnic slur. I meant there is a profound breakdown of religion in our country, as you know, in which people are not carrying out the basic teachings of morality or religion, unless those are carried out with tear gas and Mace.

CONLEY: Now, Mr. Hayden, getting back to the document again, in this document you describe a series or a wave of activities, which included the following, surrounding—

HAYDEN: Page, please?

CONLEY: Page 18, sir. Which included surrounding the Conrad Hilton, a Chicago hotel—

HAYDEN: I am sorry. Page what? Yes, go ahead.

CONLEY: Are you with me, sir?

HAYDEN: Yes.

CONLEY: Which included surrounding the Conrad Hilton, a downtown hotel, and this was in fact done during the convention, was it not?

HAYDEN: Yes. Where is that? What line? I don't see it. Page 18?

CONLEY: I am sorry, sir. I identified the wrong page. It starts on 17.

HAYDEN: Give me the first line there.

CONLEY: I am just generally paraphrasing, sir.

HAYDEN: All right. Okay, but let's read it. I know what that is; it is beautiful, but I hope you read it into the record, and let the press hear what you are reading from, instead of distorting again, as you just did.

ICHORD: Go ahead, read, Mr. Hayden. You have it before you. Read it.

HAYDEN: Well, we are giving examples of how we wanted to bring the question of poverty to the surface, because we didn't think that poverty and hunger would be dealt with by the Democratic convention. And we were giving suggestions rather than instructions, as you can see from the use of the verb "might." We are trying to give suggestions of what might happen to dramatize what we wanted, and we said,

To dramatize the demand on the urban condition, protests could focus on hundreds of the major institutions that irresponsibly contribute to urban breakdown. Welfare offices, urban renewal departments, police stations, day-labor hiring halls, large slum landlords, schools, and city hall.

Different organizations would come to Chicago prepared to carry out a specific action program. The Mississippi Freedom Democrats might want to focus attention on their lack of representation or on the failure to deal with poverty across the country.

Or a coalition of poverty-rights organizations in one region might surround the Conrad Hilton, a downtown Chicago hotel, on the morning of the twenty-sixth to greet the delegates with leaflets, demanding $15 billion to end poverty, and a breakfast menu totaling fifteen cents, the amount allotted under welfare.

At 10 A.M., the recipients might march from the Hilton to 318 West Adams to join with delegations coming from the other downtown hotels in a massive demonstration at the welfare office headquarters of Chicago. In the evening, the recipients might again return to the hotels to invite the delegates to spend the night with them in the ghetto, rather than in luxurious hotels.

ICHORD: This is suggested strategy of demonstration?

HAYDEN: This is something that we thought might be a good idea. It was a way to sort of clarify what we thought would be a good kind of protest.

ICHORD: What was your question?

HAYDEN: The question was, didn't we surround the Hilton? In fact, obviously, we didn't, because the welfare mothers chose the road of going before the Platform Committee, and in fact, the ones that I was in touch with felt it would be too dangerous to go stand in front of the Conrad Hilton, with all the police out there, so they confined their protest to speaking out forcefully before the Platform Committee, and they did not surround the Conrad Hilton, and they did not invite the delegates to live in the ghetto, and so forth.

CONLEY: Mr. Hayden, is it your testimony, then, that no group did in fact surround the Conrad Hilton?

HAYDEN: No.

CONLEY: No, that is not your testimony, or no, no group did?

HAYDEN: No one ever surrounded the Conrad Hilton, but obviously, people massed in front of it.

CONLEY: All right, sir—

HAYDEN: The police surrounded it. I am sorry.

CONLEY: The word "surrounded," though, does appear in your treatise, does it not?

HAYDEN: Treatise?

CONLEY: Advocating that the Conrad Hilton be surrounded?

HAYDEN: No, it is a matter of describing a scenario of what might be a good thing to happen. We thought it might be very good to think about welfare mothers standing all the way around, surrounding the Conrad Hilton.

CONLEY: Well, you used the word "surround," is what I am getting at.

HAYDEN: Yes, but what is wrong with picketing and surrounding a building?

CONLEY: Sir, I am not asking if there is anything wrong with it. I am just asking whether then in fact it did occur?

HAYDEN: No, it didn't.

CONLEY: All right. The only thing that did occur was a mobilization in front of the Conrad Hilton?

HAYDEN: No, no, much more than that occurred in front of the Conrad Hilton, more brutality unleashed there than I have ever seen in one night in my life. I was almost killed there.

CONLEY: Now moving on with your document, did you not also suggest that actions could concentrate or might concentrate on dozens of war targets across the city?

HAYDEN: Yes, Chicago draft boards, the downtown induction centers, the Illinois Institute of Technology, which is the nation's center for chemical and biological warfare research, and major war corporations like Dow Chemical.

CONLEY: Now were any of these things, was there any demonstration or any type of activities in connection with any of these particular suggestions?

HAYDEN: There probably were a few, but I was not aware of them, because of the pressing needs to survive the police.

CONLEY: Now, Mr. Hayden, did you not also suggest that a march be held on the International Amphitheater immediately after the first ballot, the amphitheater being the site of the Democratic national convention?

HAYDEN: Yes; August 28 would be the fifth anniversary of the March on Washington, which you will recall, was for jobs and justice. 1963.

ICHORD: Unrepresented people, Mr. Hayden?

HAYDEN: No, the march sponsored by the late Reverend Martin Luther King and other figures, and they never got their jobs or justice. We thought that it would be appropriate and symbolic on August 28, 1968, five years later, with more unemployment in the country and the black community than ever, it might be good to, as we say, and I quote, "Might begin with a massive Democratic assembly. Perhaps in Grant Park, and climax in a funeral march on the International Amphitheater, immediately after the first ballot. Such a march could be lead by retired generals, admirals, and Vietnam veterans. The funeral procession might be organized by constituencies, blacks followed by clergy, followed by women, followed by farmers and faculty and workers and resisters and so on.

"This funeral would speak for those who say that the elections represent no choice, and a complete breakdown of democracy, and those who pledged to use the fall election to expand the resistance into all sections of the American public.

"Professors engaged in war research, people who pay war taxes, recipients who let themselves be pushed around, and so forth, and so forth, and so forth. While Johnson would accept the nomination"—you see, we believed that Johnson was still in there—"a half a million people in the largest protest in the history of the country would carry caskets"—not filled with arms and weapons, like the Viet Cong did in Saigon—"symbolizing the Democratic party into the Convention area and bury them in Chicago stockyards, behind the Amphitheater."

That was certainly our hope, but this was a premature document. We didn't know what people would be for and we wrote it as a way of sort of suggesting what we thought would be a great protest.

ICHORD: What was your immediate objective, Mr. Hayden, to influence the choice of the Democratic convention?

HAYDEN: No, we knew in advance that it would be a 1964 deal all over again, where the people would be fooled into believing they had a choice, and that the Vietnam war would be brought to an end, but in fact, you would get a duplication of 1964, where as soon as the elections were over, the war would be escalated. So we calculated in advance that the Democratic convention would be the perfect time to expose the hypocrisy and chicanery of your politicians, who always are engaged in promising peace to people, while killing their sons.

And none of your Congressmen's sons are in Vietnam, but a lot of other people's sons are in Vietnam, and we thought that at the time of the—

ICHORD: Thank you, Mr. Hayden. If you will examine the record—

HAYDEN: We want to draw that out.

ICHORD: —you will find that you are in error, that there are Congressmen's sons in Vietnam.

HAYDEN: I think there are two or three, possibly, and I stand corrected—out of five hundred.

CONLEY: Now, Mr. Hayden, referring back to the earlier document that we talked about earlier, which is the "Democratic Convention Challenge"—now referring your attention to the top of page 3, did you not say in this document, "A massive confrontation with our government, the Democratic party, as it holds its convention in Chicago this summer, is being organized"?

HAYDEN: Yes, that is no secret.

CONLEY: All right, you are the one that headed—

HAYDEN: We organized it. [Ronnie Davis] and I were proj-

93

ect directors. We tried to organize a massive confrontation, but your confusion is the press's confusion in believing that confrontation can only be military. This document spells out a political confrontation in great detail.

CONLEY: Yes, sir, I am just asking you if you made the statement, if it is properly attributable to you?

HAYDEN: To myself and Rennie.

CONLEY: All right. Did you not further suggest that the Chicago demonstrations be used, and I quote you again, "to dramatize to the world the large number of people who feel unrepresented and in fact disgraced and used by our government's policies"?

HAYDEN: I don't see that, but that is certainly the way I feel about it.

CONLEY: If that statement appears there, would it be attributable to you?

HAYDEN: Yes, I just don't know where it is, but I certainly take credit for that kind of viewpoint.

CONLEY: Now turning to page 4 of that same document, sir, did you not also suggest that the local coordinating committees develop a plan to attack the Democratic convention, and did you not further suggest that—

HAYDEN: Where is this word "attack"? And what context? Page 4?

CONLEY: Page 4, the top paragraph.

HAYDEN: I will just read it until we come to it. I don't know. "The summer should be a period of intense organizing, education, and demonstrations. As local coordinating committees develop to plan the attack"—oh, yes—

the attack on the Democratic convention, they should initiate recruiting and training programs for summer organizers, who build high school draft resistance unions, organize challenges of corrupt delegates, talk with teachers, doctors, veterans, and welfare recipients about confronting the convention on a particular day, gather intelligence on delegates who will be continuously confronted and talked to during their entire stay in Chicago, speak to hundreds of local trade unions about the war and racism, build pressure in the ghetto for the removal of all Democratic party headquarters, and hold local war-crimes tribunals to expose prominent Democrats who manufacture antipersonnel bombs, poison gases, or other weapons banned by international agreement.

CONLEY: Well, in the word "attack"—after you have read the paragraph, the word "attack" is your word, it is not mine, is it?

HAYDEN: It is your meaning. It is my word.

CONLEY: I haven't put any meaning on it, sir.

HAYDEN: Of course not.

CONLEY: Now what did you mean in this statement, and I quote specifically, "build pressure in the ghetto for the removal of all Democratic party headquarters"?

HAYDEN: Well, you see, this was at a time when we were having a dialogue with sections of the black movement who were interested in the Democratic party and building an alternative political party, independent of it, and we don't think that the Democratic party has much of a right any longer to conduct the kind of campaigns that it has in the ghetto, so we thought that it shouldn't even have headquarters there.

CONLEY: My question, sir, isn't what you thought. My question is: What did you mean by "building pressure in the ghetto"? How did you propose to build this pressure?

HAYDEN: We didn't. We didn't ever propose how to do it, and we didn't ever try to do it.

CONLEY: What did you mean by it, then?

HAYDEN: What is "pressure"? Pressure: you organize people, to go to Democrats and say—

CONLEY: Yes, sir, I am asking you now for your interpretation; don't let me put mine on it.

HAYDEN: —you organize pressure, pressure is people, people going to local political hacks and telling them to deliver or get out. What could be clearer?

CONLEY: You mean you are suggesting that the pressure

95

you were talking about was for Negroes within the ghetto to go to the political hacks, as you describe them, and tell them to get out?

HAYDEN: Deliver or get out. Stop campaigning and not delivering. Something like that. I mean, we never developed it programmatically.

CONLEY: Well, this statement doesn't give an alternative, sir. It merely says pressure in the ghetto.

HAYDEN: You see, the statement does not say get them out. The statement says "build pressure in the ghetto for the removal of all Democratic party headquarters."

CONLEY: It doesn't say, "If they don't deliver." It says, to remove—

HAYDEN: I was trying to interpret it further. But the main point is that very little of this happened, and I don't even have knowledge of whether it happened. So all of this is very suggestive, and we weren't committed to any of these strategies, like organizing high school unions; we didn't speak before hundreds of trade union locals, and we didn't organize pressure in the ghetto to have Democratic party headquarters removed.

CONLEY: Now directing your attention to page 4, and the first full paragraph on that page, did you not also suggest, Mr. Hayden, that the summer should be capped by a week of demonstrations, disruptions, and marches at the Democratic national convention, clogging the streets of Chicago?

HAYDEN:

Clogging the streets of Chicago with people demanding peace, justice, and participation in government. This should be a period in which the movement projects a series of broad but concrete demands, which the vast majority of people can identify with, but which the Democratic party is shown to be unable to meet. The movement must not play into Johnson's hands by attempting to prevent the convention from assembling, a position few Americans would accept or understand. Rather, the action should build steadily through the convention week, each day escalating the de-

96

mands and the tactics, building for massive confrontation at the time of Johnson's nomination. The initial challenges and activities might involve 50,000 to 100,000 people.

The final funeral march on the convention, beginning as the first ballot is taken, should bring a half million people, demanding a choice on the issues of peace and justice, citizens who have come to 'make the democratic process work' by pinning the delegates in the International Amphitheater until a choice is presented to the American people.

A well-planned educational buildup would precede the final days of militancy. For example, alternative platform-committee hearings, challenges inside the convention as well as outside, continuous lobbying with every delegate, outdoor rallies, daily press conferences, so on and so forth.

CONLEY: Mr. Hayden, what did you mean by the use of the word "militancy"?

HAYDEN: Oh, come on. I mean I did not mean violence. I have put on the record over and over I did not mean that, and there are statements in this other document that you have read from which says that our protests should be nonviolent and legal. If you will give me the other document, I will read that to you.

(Whereupon, at 12:03 P.M., the subcommittee recessed, to reconvene at 2:00 P.M., the same day.)

＊　　　　＊　　　　＊

CONLEY: Mr. Hayden, I think at the time of the recess you have been asked a question about a quote attributable to you which appeared in this publication, "Discussion of the Democratic Convention Challenge."

I think the last question that we asked you was, Is there in fact a quotation in there, words to the effect, on page 4 in the first full paragraph, that, "The summer should be capped by a week of demonstrations, disruptions, and marches at the Democratic national convention, clogging the streets of Chicago."

97

HAYDEN: No, that would be a total erroneous understanding.

CONLEY: Are those words in that?

HAYDEN: There are some of the words you have taken out of the sentence, out of the paragraph, and out of the document. You have done it in such a way as to totally alter the meaning.

CONLEY: I have not asked you what the meaning was. I have asked you if the words appear.

HAYDEN: I was putting my point in your reference.

CONLEY: Do the words "demonstrations, disruptions, marches at the Democratic national convention clogging the streets of Chicago," do those words appear in that article?

HAYDEN: They appear but not as a sentence.

CONLEY: They do appear?

HAYDEN: They appear in the context of a sentence.

CONLEY: Now, sir, I will be pleased to hear your explanation.

HAYDEN: I have already gone into that.

CONLEY: All right. Then we will move on if we may. On the same page does not the following statement appear, that one of your policies or plans was "pinning the delegates in the National Amphitheater until the choice is presented to the American people"?

HAYDEN: Yes, I read that to you before—

CONLEY: This does appear.

HAYDEN: —as part of the sentence. I read the entire sentence before.

ASHBROOK: This I assume is nonviolently and peacefully you would pin them in there. How is this done?

HAYDEN: I don't want to bore you, but I think I read to you an extensive description of the funeral march on the Democratic convention before.

ASHBROOK: You don't pin people in a funeral march, do you?

98

HAYDEN: In effect, by coming down there to bury the coffins in the stockyard the convention hall would be surrounded. Obviously, we would not be able to literally pin or literally prevent the convention people from coming and going because obviously they have access that the police can allow for them.

ASHBROOK: Do you think all the people who were there knew that?

HAYDEN: In our permits which we submitted in writing over and over again, which are public documents, we indicated what we meant by this. We indicated with maps and with descriptions where we wanted to go to the Amphitheater, where we wanted our rally to be held. At no time did we submit plans or organize on the sort of preposterous basis of literally being able to pin or enclose people in a place.

CONLEY: Then, sir, is not the use of the word "pin" a poor choice of words?

HAYDEN: You may think so.

CONLEY: I am asking you.

HAYDEN: I think that our meaning is conveyed in this document adequately. I will defend the use of this word or any other word.

CONLEY: Mr. Hayden, another question in the same area. This is the only paragraph that I read in this particular article that we have been reading from today where it is not couched in the terms "might," or a proposal; it is couched in a more specific way, almost to the point of saying "shall." I don't know whether you actually used the word "shall" in there, but it is not suggested as a possibility, at least this particular paragraph does not read as a possibility as some of the other paragraphs do. It reads as a position.

HAYDEN: Well, at the beginning, you see, we divided into spring, summer, and convention time. We said that the summer should be capped by a week of demonstrations, etc.

What we were saying here is that we prefer this thing that we write about to come about.

CONLEY: But you didn't say the summer might be capped by, you said "the summer should be capped by."

HAYDEN: So what. I obviously said that. All I am saying is that is exactly what you want me to say. It is what Mr. Davis and I proposed should happen, but I just want you to keep in mind that since this was written in January or February it was really meant to provoke discussion. Our own concept of what should be done and how it should be done changed over the next several months several times, depending on what the new situation was in the country.

CONLEY: Weren't these actions which you proposed, Mr. Hayden, actually planned to disrupt the convention?

HAYDEN: No.

CONLEY: Was this the purpose?

HAYDEN: No: If you will let me give an extended answer, having said no, I will be glad to try to clear that up. I don't want to go over past ground, but I have said several times and shown you in documents that you have in your possession, that our purpose was political.

None of us thought that our purpose would be served by violence. We wanted the largest number possible of people to come to Chicago. We knew that the threat of violence would keep people away. Faced with what we considered to be the violence, the lack of permits, we decided we had to go to Chicago anyway and take our chances.

But at no time did we want that to happen for a very serious political reason. I think that most people in this country respect the right of the Democratic party or any other party to hold a convention and decide on its candidates and decide on its policies. We are not questioning their right to do that.

We are questioning their authority, their legitimacy, their status in our eyes and, essentially, the morality of what they are doing. That is the point. If it was going to be disrupted, as I have said in speeches and in writing, during convention week, I always believed that the disruption would occur by the military machinery turning against itself.

You see, you had a situation where an agent from one agency was arresting another agent; they were spying on each other, arresting each other. I remember one day in Lincoln Park, an officer from one agency arrested another fellow who was taking a picture because he thought it was a demonstrator taking a picture of himself.

It turned out there were just two people from different agencies spying on each other.

As you saw that momentum build up, due to the presence of so many troops in the city, not exactly knowing what they were there for; and you saw the methods practiced inside the convention hall in which a substantial minority of the delegates felt—whether you agree with them or not, a substantial minority of the delegates felt that the entire operation was being manipulated and controlled undemocratically by the Johnson administration; there were times inside the convention, on the floor of the convention, that mass violence almost broke out as a result of what one television broadcaster called the thugs who seemed to be on the convention floor.

There were times when the chairman of the delegation moved that the convention stop and leave town. One U. S. Senator discussed from the podium the Gestapo tactics outside and was attacked in obscene language by Mayor Daley.

ICHORD: Were you inside the convention, Mr. Hayden?

HAYDEN: No.

ICHORD: You are testifying from hearsay?

HAYDEN: I am testifying from what I saw on television. I thought there were points during that week in which the convention would simply fold up. I saw the Democratic party

GLENDALE COLLEGE LIBRARY

eating itself because there is no security in this kind of military defense that the United States and that the convention had.

You cannot secure yourself from people by building more and more barbed wire and getting more spies and infiltrators and more sophisticated weapons. All you do is make yourself fundamentally insecure.

That is how I thought the convention would disrupt itself.

CONLEY: Mr. Hayden—

HAYDEN: And it almost did. It almost ended before it came to the nominations.

CONLEY: In that vein I am sure you are familiar with the article which appeared in the December issue of *Esquire* dealing with you: "Tom Hayden—Will He Overcome?" or something to that effect.

HAYDEN: You are probably far more familiar with it.

CONLEY: There is a paragraph in it. I am not attributing this as a quote to you, but apparently it is an assessment of the reporters talking with you. It appears in the next to the last page of this article. In the third column it says, "This is the real point of Chicago. Hayden saw it as an ideal opportunity to provide a confrontation with the police in full view of the television cameras. Enough bloody heads and some people might get mad enough to cross over the line and put themselves in opposition to become 'radicalized.' "

HAYDEN: I'm sorry, did you have something further to ask or what?

CONLEY: I am asking you in view of your answer here that you were not intending to disrupt the convention, if this impression you created with this reporter at least would indicate otherwise.

HAYDEN: I never talked to this reporter during or very far before the convention. His opinion about me is quite similar to yours. I can't help that, but I would like to read to you my own statement about the subject which appeared in *Rat*. The *Rat* is a publication—

CONLEY: I don't mind your reading the statement if you will answer my original question. You say this is not a fair assessment?

HAYDEN: Of course it is not a fair assessment. It is contradictory to everything I have said to you all day.

CONLEY: Mr. Hayden—

HAYDEN: Let me tell you my position.

CONLEY: Just a second. Let me ask you this.

ICHORD: The Chair is not going to require the witness to comment on the assessment by the reporter. If he wishes to do so I will recognize the purpose in doing it.

HAYDEN: I would like to read a couple of things that I wrote which were distributed in the closest thing to an official statement of what organizers of the demonstration were planning. In one article about the police preparations for the convention I said the following:

The main thrust of their schemes revealed the mentality of the bully attempting to win by force what persuasion has failed to do, acceptance of a rigid political decision. Their strategy is to frighten people into surrendering their right to dissent, to demonstrate, to take to the streets.

Jack Mabley of *Chicago's American* wrote on July 25 that Chicago has established the reputation of being "an uptight city with tough police." That has achieved a sobering effect, he said, on potential peace demonstrators "who are willing to risk a slight bump on the head or a twisted arm or a night in the cooler in New York or San Francisco, but not a skull fracture in Chicago."

The purpose, therefore, according to Mabley, of the police preparation was to develop a strong movement to warn young hippies and yippies away from Chicago.

Then I said the following:

The sadistic and provocative element is represented within the Chicago Police Department. They are expected to use their clubs, especially at night, against small groups of peaceniks. The Mobilization Committee has asked the Justice Department to investigate the existence of a right-wing conspiracy within the Police Department to take advantage of the demonstrations to provoke violence.

The Justice Department has refused to make such an investigation.

Then I go on to say,

The strategic problems of the Establishment are immense, consisting of contradictions between the need for security and the need for political image.

Security demands a militarized Chicago and ringing the Amphitheater with troops. Too great a military presence threatens to alienate young people, McCarthy supporters, undermine confidence in the U.S. government everywhere, and open the administration to the ridicule of its critics.

Thus on the strategic level the government is already working from a political disadvantage.

Then I go on and on and on and I say,

The Mobilization has asked for the withdrawal of all military forces from the vicinity of our demonstrations. They can carry on routine functions but the Mobilization wants none of their protection, which inevitably means police provocation and brutality.

However, if the authorities insist on ringing demonstrators everywhere with menacing troops, then they will be creating a full military occupation of Chicago. Thus even peaceful and orderly demonstrations will be dramatic experiences and will show a widening gap between the people with grievances and their supposed political representatives.

When not demonstrating, we can laugh from beaches and turn to more serious topics while they protect their government and private property. In making Chicago safe for their 'democracy' they will show others that this democracy is unsafe for human beings.

Again we understand if violence occurs it will be because of the negligence and brutality of national and local authorities. They have called us disrupters, refused us marching permits, bluffed through shows of strength, refused to clean out the vigilante reactionaries operating within the police force, and above all resisted all peaceful pressures for change.

We do not welcome the beating or killing of even a single

member of our movement. We do not reduce individuals to cannon fodder as the warmakers do. We do not risk our people to 'radicalize' others, but we know the serious struggle cannot begin without each individual preparing to accept jail or suffering as a price.

We will not be intimidated into surrendering our rights to protest. We cannot allow an unjust law and order to be imposed by police methods.

ICHORD: This is a writing of yours, Mr. Hayden, but what served as a basis of the reporter's assessment?

HAYDEN: I don't know the basis of his assessment. I am saying that what I have just read is from the convention document of the *Rat*. It was the closest thing to a semiofficial position by myself and other organizers. I tried to point out that the convention was in danger of disrupting itself because of its security preparations, not because of us.

These preparations can't go hand in hand with a peaceful convention. I tried to indicate that I don't really believe in this theory that the *Esquire* magazine article ascribes to me, that somehow you move people to the left or radicalize them by letting them get beat over the head by policemen.

ICHORD: You don't feel that pinning the delegates in the Amphitheater would help to alleviate these undesirable situations which you attribute to the convention?

HAYDEN: In our proposals, which began in late spring and early summer in the city of Chicago, which I can bring out to you complete with maps, we can show how it was possible and how we proposed to the city how they could station whatever number of troops they wanted around the Amphitheater, guarantee coming and going to all the delegates, and still allow a march to come to the Amphitheater which was the site of what we thought was a national tragedy, and have the marchers go around the Amphitheater and have an enormous rally outside of it. It would be possible both to have a convention and have such a demonstration. In other words, the coalition between the riots of the conventioners, you folks, and our riots, did not have to come off.

ASHBROOK: If they played it your way?

HAYDEN: Right. Do you really think that the hippies and yippies and people like myself are coming to Chicago, with the kind of composition of our movement that we have, that we seriously planned to take on the Police Department, charge through the doors, and tear up the convention?

That is ridiculous. That is what I tried to say earlier about why I didn't think violence was meaningful in Chicago. I don't believe in this sort of throwing around the concept of violence loosely, and I did not believe, and I never believed that it would be possible, quite apart from whether it was desirable—I didn't think it was desirable either—but I knew from the beginning it was not possible to carry through on some kind of concept of invading or disrupting the convention.

What I wanted to know is why, with all your police force and intelligence agencies, you weren't as smart as we were? I think you are as smart as we were, so you turn the thing into a gigantic myth. Anybody knows that LSD in the water is not a real threat, it cannot work.

A little consultation with a doctor or scientist would straighten you out. With the Pentagon and state and local troops on the scene to figure things out for months in advance I cannot understand why you thought it was possible, with minimum police protection for us to somehow enter and turn the convention upside down.

I cannot understand it. Therefore, I think someone somewhere decided that it would be a good political thing to have all those troops in Chicago.

ICHORD: You are saying "You," Mr. Hayden. I think you have to remember that Mr. Ashbrook is a member of the Republican party.

HAYDEN: Right. I was trying to draw him out.

CONLEY: Mr. Hayden, in this same vein let me ask you about something which appeared in *Guardian,*[*] the official organ of the Central Committee of the Communist Party of Cuba in its issue of September 8, 1968, page 12. They published the text of an August 28 telephone interview with Michael Klonsky, national secretary of SDS. My first question would be do you know Michael Klonsky?

HAYDEN: Yes.

CONLEY: This interview was apparently held with Mr. Klonsky by telephone from Havana to Chicago during the course of the convention. Mr. Klonsky was asked this question: "What can you tell us about the present situation in Chicago?"

Mr. Klonsky's answer was as follows:

We have been fighting in the streets for four days. Many of our people have been beaten up and many of them are in jail, but we are winning. We pushed the police out of Grant Park and the people are still in the streets. They are going to be in the streets all night and we are going to do anything we can to stop this farce, the Democratic convention, which is taking place in Chicago. The people are committed to carry on this fight not only in Chicago but throughout the United States. We are going to go back to the hotel and down to the park again and are going to carry on the fight all night until the Convention is over. The police have been very brutal and a lot of people have been shot and a lot of people have been beaten up but the young people have committed themselves to fight and they are fighting very bravely.

HAYDEN: What was the date of this? When was this interview?

CONLEY: The interview was on August 28.

HAYDEN: How could that be? I see it is on the twenty-eighth. Then there is something curious about the interview because on that day the convention was virtually ended.

---

[*] Conley apparently means *Granma,* the official organ of the Central Committee of the Communist Party of Cuba. *The Guardian* is an independent radical news weekly published in New York City.

ICHORD: The date of the convention was August 26 through 29, was it not?

HAYDEN: The nominations and the real finish was the night of the twenty-eighth. There was no demonstration or activity on the twenty-ninth.

CONLEY: This is in reference to the twenty-eighth.

HAYDEN: All right. What is your point?

CONLEY: My question is, Did you have any conversations with Mr. Klonsky in Chicago at the time of this interview?

HAYDEN: No.

CONLEY: You know nothing about what he told them?

HAYDEN: What he told the Cubans?

CONLEY: Yes.

HAYDEN: No. This is the first I knew about this. I knew that a very funny thing happened. A Cuban radio called up the Mobilization office in the middle of the convention and asked what was happening and Dellinger picked up the phone. That is the only time I knew about it. I think somebody else called from some other foreign country.

CONLEY: This particular answer to the question would indicate that whoever Mr. Klonsky was speaking for had no intention of letting the Democratic convention be completed. Don't you read it that way?

HAYDEN: I don't quite read it that way.

CONLEY: "We have no intention of letting this Convention finish or this farce"? I think he calls it the farce.

HAYDEN: "We are going to do anything we can to stop this farce which is taking place in Chicago." Stop the farce; does that mean to you invasion of the convention? What does it mean? Certainly by that time it did not mean invasion of the convention, August 28.

CONLEY: He says you are going to do anything.

HAYDEN: What does that mean?

CONLEY: That gives you a lot of options. That is what I am asking you, sir.

HAYDEN: A lot or none. We have the reports on what was done according to the Chicago Police Department. As far as I know a lot of things were not done—there were no weapons confiscated. There were one or two. There was a McCarthy card among the weapons, there was a bag of urine or some sticks.

In terms of those realities I think this phrase, "We are going to do anything we can," should be judged in terms of the actual facts of the matter. You saw what they did. So I don't know what your point is.

CONLEY: My point is, sir, that he indicates in that interview that he was willing to do anything to stop the farce.

HAYDEN: Did he?

CONLEY: I asked you if that is not what the interview said.

HAYDEN: Obviously, he must have decided there were things he should not do.

ICHORD: Mr. Counsel, the witness was not present at the interview.

HAYDEN: I don't even know if it is a correct interview.

CONLEY: Mr. Hayden, do you of your own knowledge know of anyone who was shot?

HAYDEN: Yes, killed.

CONLEY: In Chicago?

HAYDEN: Yes.

CONLEY: Who?

HAYDEN: An American Indian from one of the Dakotas whose name appears in the document. I can't remember his name. He was described in the Chicago papers as a yippie-clad person. He was shot and killed about the 22, 23, or 24, something like that. Allegedly, he had pulled a gun out of his bag and shot at point-blank range at the officer, plainclothes officer, I believe, who had him. That is like two feet away.

ICHORD: Were you there?

HAYDEN: No. This is the report of the police. Somehow it missed this policeman.

CONLEY: Was this at the convention?

HAYDEN: At the beginning. Just when people were coming to town. It threw extreme fear into people around the country. We had a lot of phone calls. The news went out around the country there had been the first clash between a hippie and a policeman.

I can read to you from page 83.*

One incident that contributed to the week's uncertainty and the demonstrators' edginess was the August 22 killing of a seventeen-year-old American Indian. Jerome Johnson, from Sioux Falls, South Dakota, was shot to death by police at North Avenue and Wells Street just a few blocks southwest of the park.

A police detective said they fired their guns when the fleeing youth identified as a yippie fired a 32-caliber revolver at them. The shooting caused one of the marshal-trainers to say, "We don't want to go overboard in ascribing malevolent intentions to the police, but obviously things are going to be very rough here. We have to be prepared."

That is the only person that I know of that was killed in connection with the Chicago convention. But I know a lot of shots were fired over people's heads and that the situation was one in which some people could have been killed very easily.

CONLEY: Let me direct your attention back to the Havana interview wherein Mr. Klonsky apparently relates—

HAYDEN: He writes some people were killed some nights ago. I don't know whether Klonsky said that or whether the Cubans made it up. All I know is what it says here. It is reproduced and apparently was said on August 28. Again, I don't understand your point except that this statement of his is in error, whether it is a Cuban error or a Klonsky error.

CONLEY: Or an SDS error?

HAYDEN: SDS error? SDS does not make errors. We don't

* Cited in the Walker Report.

have such an organization. It is not capable of making any kind of decision.

CONLEY: Mr. Hayden, were you at a meeting held in Chicago by the National Mobilization Committee on August 4 of this year?

HAYDEN: I don't know. Explain the meeting and I will try to answer.

CONLEY: Maybe I can refresh your memory. Was it suggested at that meeting, if you were there—

HAYDEN: Where was it and who was at it?

CONLEY: 407 South Dearborn. It was suggested at that meeting by Rennie Davis, speaking for the steering committee, of which you are a member, that on the day of the nomination, Wednesday, the twenty-eighth of August, you would have a massive march to the Amphitheater.

HAYDEN: There was always that proposal, not simply of Rennie Davis, but all the officers of the Mobilization that we were going to march to the Amphitheater.

CONLEY: Mr. Davis was speaking for the steering committee, was he not?

HAYDEN: I don't know whether he was speaking for the steering committee or simply speaking as a project director.

CONLEY. This did, in fact, occur then?

HAYDEN: Let me see what you are reading from here. It will just take a second.

All I see, sir, is the following:

"The discussion moved to the massive march proposal, analyzing the various routes to the Amphitheater and the length of the different routes. Dave"—that is, Dellinger—"pointed out calling for an action not related to the Amphitheater on the twenty-eighth was ignoring the natural magnetism of the place, that the media would be at the Amphitheater and the necessity of having the military surround a mass of people at a Democratic convention would lend political content to the action. There was a discussion of the possibility of proceeding in the face of a curfew, threat, or denial of the permit. It was pointed out that the Mobilization has rallied people before without a permit and that insistence on stating an announced aim made a strong bargaining position in negotiating a permit."

I am trying to find what you say Rennie said. I don't find that. I will read everything, but—

CONLEY: If you are on page 2, this is all said by Mr. Davis.

HAYDEN: That is what I can't understand.

CONLEY: Mine says, "Proposed scenario recommended by the steering committee represented by Rennie Davis."

HAYDEN: That is absurd the way you are reading it. The scenario is under where it says proposed scenario, then the rest are notes from the meeting, from the discussion made by whoever the secretary was.

Here it is:

The day of the nominations, Wednesday, August 28, will see the massive march. At about 3:00 P.M. marchers will gather north of the loop, proceed to the central downtown business area to the Amphitheater in a specified one-mile area along Halstead, go to the Amphitheater. Demonstrators can hold a vigil, picnic, creative theater, or rally.

When it concludes, the marchers will leave as a unit to the Grant Park band shell, where they will disperse. This event, which will be aided by experienced marshals, will include a teach-in for the troops, stressing that our differences are not with them.

That was the proposal.

ICHORD: The proposal made after the application for the march to the Amphitheater was applied for?

HAYDEN: Yes. This was in the course of our negotiations with the city, if you want to call them negotiations. I would say it was sort of a one-way monologue with the city listening to us but not responding until a couple of days before the convention.

CONLEY: Now, in connection with the paragraph that you were reading a while ago and directing your attention specifically to the top of page 4—

HAYDEN: What is the first word on 4, I don't have a number.

CONLEY: "Insistence."

HAYDEN: I saw that wink in your eye. You want me to read down there?

CONLEY: No, I just want to know did there not occur the possibility that the city of Chicago would not permit a march against the Democratic convention, and was it not suggested by the persons in attendance that you would make this march on the Democratic convention whether or not a permit was issued?

HAYDEN: It was always our position, stated over and over in the media: You don't need a House committee to investigate this question—that we thought that we were within our legal rights to march to the Amphitheater, that a parade permit was merely a technical instrument that a city is supposed to use to allow people to conduct legal activities, but this parade permit was being stalled and held back by the city authorities because they did not want people to come to Chicago.

They never negotiated with us in good faith. Many people high in the Democratic party know that. They were the losers. At the last moment they came through—after we had taken them to court—with some proposals which did not meet the substance of our request at all.

A judge who was Mayor Daley's law partner, Judge Lynch, very nicely named, denied our application and said that we could not have a permit. We said at that point that we would march, regardless, to the Amphitheater. We knew that it was in violation of this judge's ruling.

We were prepared to accept whatever consequence came from that. We obviously knew that this would certainly not interrupt the Democratic convention. In fact, we knew that we would not even get out of downtown without a permit, and we didn't on August 28. The police simply made it clear that they would block all arteries leading south to the Amphitheater, and they did.

We were bottled up in Grant Park for the whole day. We attempted to march, led by Dave Dellinger. We got to the police lines and stopped.

CONLEY: Specifically was it not Mr. Robert Greenblatt who made the statement that if the curfew were imposed it should be disobeyed?

HAYDEN: It could very well have been Greenblatt. I don't recall exactly. Greenblatt is a responsible officer of the organization.

CONLEY: I will ask you to refer to the minutes.

HAYDEN: The minutes do say Greenblatt. I will say it myself, Dellinger said it himself. Davis said it. Everybody agreed on that. As you read the notes you will see it was passed.

CONLEY: Was it not at this meeting of August 4 that it was agreed Vernon Grizzard would be in charge of the marshals?

HAYDEN: Yes, we wanted Vernon to be in charge of the marshals. Yes, you are right, in the minutes it was accepted.

It is interesting that you don't mention the other names because obviously you are interested in this Budapest conference that Vernon traveled to. I want to get back to this business in Paris with the Vietnamese as soon as possible to set the record straight about what our relations are with the Vietnamese and what Vernon was doing.

CONLEY: Let us get back to something else first, Mr. Hayden, because you brought it up: *Rat*. You were reading from this a moment ago. Would you be kind enough to explain to the Committee what *Rat* is?

HAYDEN: Well, it is self-evident. It is an underground newspaper. It is published in New York and it is called the *Rat*.

ICHORD: Published by whom, Mr. Hayden?

HAYDEN: The *Rat* staff. Editor, Jeffrey Shero; hero workers, Jeff Gerth, Martha Kusic; office, guru, Sybil Dryden; maps, Michael Klare; graphics, hobo graphics, Rick Meyerwitz; advertising manager, Marvin Grafton.

ICHORD: Is this the official publication of any organization?

HAYDEN: Published biweekly by Rat Publishing, 201 East Fourth Street, New York, New York. Application for mail at second-class postage rates, etc., member of Liberation News Service and Underground Press Syndicate.

CONLEY: Is *Rat* not in fact an organ of the SDS, Students for a Democratic Society?

HAYDEN: No. SDS has an organ called *New Left Notes.*

CONLEY: I am aware of that, but is not also *Rat* an organ of the same society?

HAYDEN: You will have to ask the society. As far as I know, it never has been.

CONLEY: Since you had previously been an officer of that society I thought you might be able to shed some light on the question.

HAYDEN: I have. Whether you like it or not that is the light that is shed. It is not connected to SDS.

CONLEY: Mr. Hayden, was this particular issue also known as the Demonstrators' Guidebook or Handbook?

HAYDEN: It says "Convention special. Lyndon's birthday follies. Inside, maps and muck." I will tell you about it.

CONLEY: I am not interested in it—

HAYDEN: Rennie Davis and I wrote several articles explaining our political philosophy and information that we thought people should have if they were to come to demonstrate at Chicago, but it was not an official organ of SDS, or the Mobilization, or anyone else. That is what I said before, this is the closest thing to a sort of official recording of the views of myself and Rennie as project directors of the Mobilization.

115

It includes maps of the Chicago Loop and different targets where you can demonstrate in the city of Chicago. The maps are introduced by the following statement:

> In order to avoid unnecessary violence and bloodshed it will be crucial to hold demonstrations at locations other than the International Amphitheater, where the concentration of police and National Guard is very high.
>
> The following maps contain information about possible alternate demonstration sites throughout Chicago. Such information should enhance our mobility and assist in the formation and execution of relatively safe demonstration strategies by different groups.

Then it has where all the rulers of America are located in the city, different buildings that they have, banks, insurance companies, that sort of thing. And it has a map of the Amphitheater area as well. It has an article on Mayor Daley, not very flattering.

CONLEY: Was it stated at the meeting on August 4 that 100,000 copies of this special edition of *Rat* would be available?

HAYDEN: It might have been, but we decided on a smaller number. I think it was 30,000.

CONLEY: I will refer you to your notes again on page 3.

HAYDEN: Whatever the notes say—I am sure you are reading them correctly—we came out with 30,000 instead of 100,000.

CONLEY: Now, Mr. Hayden, if we may move on, in connection with the National Mobilization Committee to End the War in Vietnam, is it not a fact that the following people whom I am going to name were also invited to attend meetings of the administrative committee or the steering committee of the National Mobilization Committee—

HAYDEN: Excuse me. Would it be possible for Mr. Davis to come up just to be a consultant to me on these questions of past meetings?

116

ICHORD: The Chair realizes, Mr. Hayden, that no one's memory is perfect. If you do not recall—

HAYDEN: As long as it is understood that I am not trying to hide anything under a bed I will be glad to tell you when I can't remember things.

CONLEY: Okay. Did you want to have him come up?

HAYDEN: I would like him to come up. If the Chair thinks it is unnecessary—

ICHORD: If he feels he wants to consult with him, I think Mr. Davis is close enough there, if you feel you have to consult with him feel free to do so.

CONLEY: In order that I can make this as short as possible, you see the general tenor of my questions, sir.

Other people invited to attend meetings of the planning committee of the National Mobilization Committee other than yourself: Mr. Herbert Bleich.

HAYDEN: Are you reading from some list that I have also?

CONLEY: It is from a composite list.

HAYDEN: I don't know who Herbert Bleich is.

ICHORD: The witness stated he did not know who Herbert Bleich is.

HAYDEN: As far as I know, I don't know unless you are mispronouncing the name.

CONLEY: That is why I am spelling it for you, sir, B-l-e-i-c-h.

HAYDEN: As far as I know I have never met such a person.

CONLEY: He has been identified by this committee as being affiliated with the Progressive Labor party, if that helps you in any way.

HAYDEN: No, that does not clear up anything.

CONLEY: The second name, Stokeley Carmichael, Black Panther advocate, who is now involved with the Black Panther organization.

HAYDEN: What was the question, was he attending meetings?

CONLEY: Was he invited to attend meetings, and did he attend meetings?

HAYDEN: He may have been invited. He did not attend.

CONLEY: Any of the meetings you attended?

HAYDEN: No.

CONLEY: Kip Dawson of the Socialist Workers party?

HAYDEN: He may have, but I don't know him. I don't know whether he was at a meeting.

CONLEY: I have been told that Kip Dawson is a female rather than a male.

HAYDEN: Well, that shows I don't know him.

CONLEY: Abe Fineglass of the Communist party.

HAYDEN: Abe Fineglass of the Communist party? Is he listed as such? I have heard the name. I think he is a trade unionist. Whether he is a member of the Communist party, I don't know. I don't know if he attended any meetings.

CONLEY: Paul Freedman, New York State Youth Director of the Communist party.

HAYDEN: I don't know him.

CONLEY: Jesse Gray.

HAYDEN: As far as I know, Jesse Gray never attended meetings. I do know Jesse Gray somewhat.

CONLEY: Fred Halsted of the Socialist Workers party.

HAYDEN: Yes, Fred attended some meetings. I think he is an officer of the Mobilization anyway.

CONLEY: Lou Jones of the Young Socialist Alliance.

HAYDEN: He was present at some meetings. I forget which ones. You see, they didn't go for the action because they have a Trotskyist outlook. They don't believe the Democratic party is legitimate at all, so they didn't want any demonstration whatsoever in the city of Chicago. So they did not participate very heavily in our planning.

CONLEY: Bettina Aptheker, of the Communist party.

HAYDEN: I know Bettina just a little bit. I know her daddy better. I don't believe she was involved in the meetings.

118

CONLEY: Her daddy, I take it, is Herbert?

HAYDEN: You guessed it.

CONLEY: Sam Marcey, also known as Sam Blan, Trotskyist World Workers party.

HAYDEN: I don't know—my saying I don't know these people does not prove anything. They may be around my bed. They may have been at meetings.

CONLEY: I understand. Jack Odell, also known as Hunter Pitts Odell, of the Communist party.

HAYDEN: No idea.

CONLEY: Harry Ring, of the Socialist Workers party.

HAYDEN: Harry Ring I met in Cuba once. He may have attended a Mobilization meeting. But as I said, these people, the Trotskyists, were against the action. So he couldn't have participated very heavily.

ICHORD: Is the Trotskyite against—

HAYDEN: For the reason I said, they don't believe—; you see, if you demonstrate outside the convention they think this assumes you believe in the validity of the two-party system and they don't believe in its validity, so they didn't think there should be any demonstration there because it would be misleading the American people. I'm not a Trotskyist, myself, but I may have done injustice to their position.

CONLEY: José Ristourcci.

HAYDEN: No idea.

CONLEY: Jack Spiegel.

HAYDEN: Spiegel, yes, Spiegel was in Chicago.

CONLEY: Arnold Johnson of the Communist party.

HAYDEN: Arnold Johnson I know slightly. He was at least at one meeting representing the Communist party. Other than that I don't remember. I don't even know if he was in Chicago.

CONLEY: Mr. Hayden, is it not a fact that you have made trips to foreign countries to meet with foreign Communist officials?

119

HAYDEN: Yes.

CONLEY: Did you not sign up as a delegate to attend the Soviet-controlled Communist World Youth Festival held in Helsinki, Finland, in 1962?

HAYDEN: I'm glad you brought that up.

CONLEY: Remember, all I have asked you is did you sign up.

HAYDEN: Just read it again. That is beautiful.

CONLEY: Did you sign up to make that trip?

HAYDEN: Say the whole question as you said it.

CONLEY: Did you not sign up as a delegate to attend the Soviet-controlled Communist World Youth Festival held in Helsinki, Finland, in 1962?

HAYDEN: This is an occasion where I was a dupe of the CIA, which controlled the National Student Association at the time. I was enticed by them to go to Helsinki as part of a little anti-Communist group that would try to make trouble for the Communists. I thought it would be a good trip, nice to have my way paid by whoever was paying it, probably the State Department or the CIA. Only at the last moment other problems here in this country prevented me from going. But I was going to carry Old Glory right into the heart of communism at that time. Now that can be proven by any number of CIA agents, former student leaders, organizers of the trip, or what have you.

CONLEY: My question was, Did you originally sign up to go?

HAYDEN: I signed up not to go as a delegate, I don't think. I signed up to go as sort of a Radio Free America, or whatever we thought we were doing. We were going to go over there. I was a member of the group of Americans who were going to put out a little newspaper to tell the truth to all the Communists.

CONLEY: Mr. Hayden, although you did not go and you have offered us an explanation as to why you did not go, is it not a fact that you have since that time indicated that you wished you had had the opportunity to attend that festival?

HAYDEN: Yes, I would have liked to have seen it but I was accused of being a Communist here and had to fight that one out. That was when the parent organization of SDS threw SDS out back in 1962. That is in the history books.

CONLEY: Mr. Hayden, in December of 1965, did you not travel to North Vietnam together with Staughton Lynd and Herbert Aptheker to attend meetings with such Communist officials as Premier Van Dong?

HAYDEN: Right. But the purpose was not to attend meetings with the premier of North Vietnam in particular. The purpose was—

CONLEY: My question was "with such Communist officials."

HAYDEN: Yes. I was trying to answer the question. The purpose was to try to understand the outlook on peace and war that the other side held. We wanted to interview a variety of people in North Vietnam.

CONLEY: On that trip in December, 1965, did you meet with Colonel Ha Van Lau, who was mentioned here earlier this morning, who at that time I believe was liaison officer of the North Vietnamese on the International Control Commission?

HAYDEN: He was the liaison, I believe, between the North Vietnamese Army and the International Control Commission which was established by the Geneva Agreements. We heard from him a detailed analysis of their negotiating position and their view of the Geneva Agreements both in the past and in the future. We printed that interview in a book which we published, *The Other Side*, in 1966.

CONLEY: Mr. Hayden, with regard to this trip, were you not aware of the fact that Herbert Aptheker of the National Committee, member of the Communist party, U.S.A., received the original invitation from the North Vietnamese and was told to bring two persons with him?

121

HAYDEN: That is the first time I have heard that version of it but I am getting used to these kinds of doctored versions. I'll tell you what happened. Herbert Aptheker, whom I had not met before I partook in a debate, attended a conference in Helsinki in the summer of 1965 or early fall, which was one of the first conferences in Europe that I believe a North Vietnamese delegation came to since the beginning of the bombing in early 1965.

They asked Aptheker if he would like to visit North Vietnam, which is a Communist country, he being a Communist party official of the United States. He said he would be interested. They said they would like to also have acquaintance and contact with people in the emerging peace movement in the United States who were not in the Communist party, who were not Communists. So he came back to do that. He contacted Prof. Staughton Lynd, whom he knew slightly, but who at that time was one of the most widely acknowledged leaders of the protest against the war. Professor Lynd thought it over and decided he would like to see North Vietnam, and Professor Lynd asked if he could select a third person, and he selected myself. We had been friends in Atlanta and lived in the same community and had sort of been in contact for a couple of years. So we went with Dr. Aptheker, as you say, in December.

CONLEY: Mr. Hayden, it is not your understanding then that Mr. Aptheker, in fact, initially invited Carl Oglesby of the SDS as well as leaders of the Student Nonviolent Coordinating Committee to make this trip before he extended the invitation to Professor Lynd and yourself?

HAYDEN: Not that I know of, but you can ask him. I'm sure that other people were considered but I don't know who they were.

CONLEY: Let me ask you this: Do you recall having a conversation with a reporter from the *Village Voice,* a newspaper reporter by the name of Jack Newfield?

HAYDEN: I recall more than one conversation.

CONLEY: Do you recall a conversation with him where you indicated these were the facts, that Oglesby and somebody from SNCC were invited initially and they were not willing to go?

HAYDEN: I don't remember who was invited. I was not particularly involved in that. You will have to ask somebody else. Even if it were true I would be glad to acknowledge it. I just don't know whether it is true.

CONLEY: Do you recall in this conversation with Mr. Newfield that he advised you to contact the *New York Times?*

HAYDEN: No, I don't recall.

CONLEY: Did you contact the *New York Times?*

HAYDEN: Before going to Hanoi?

CONLEY: Before or after you got back?

HAYDEN: Yes.

CONLEY: Did you make a proposal to them to give them an exclusive story on your trip to Hanoi on the condition they play up the role of Staughton Lynd and down the role of Communist party official Herbert Aptheker?

HAYDEN: That is a joke.

CONLEY: I am asking the question.

HAYDEN: I answered it. Do you think the *New York Times* would agree to such a bargain?

CONLEY: That is not the question, sir, whether they agreed to it. The question is, did you propose it?

HAYDEN: There never was such a proposal. We would not be insane enough to think that the *New York Times* was, you know, capable of that kind of reasoning. I think we had the following problem. There was going to be a critical problem of publicity. We were aware that a story might break at any time, especially when we were away from the United States and we would not be able to talk to the press. We would be in China or Vietnam or somewhere out of contact with the American press. So we decided to leave behind separate statements, each of us, and after much debate we decided that we would agree on the strategy of telling the reporter from the *New York Times* essentially what was happening with the understanding that if the story was about to break he could break it. He just wrote whatever he wanted to write. The idea that they were boosting Staughton Lynd and downplaying Herbert Aptheker I cannot understand.

CONLEY: My question was not, did the *Times* do this; my question was, did you propose this to the *Times?*

HAYDEN: Of cousre not.

CONLEY: You have no knowledge of any of the other two people who made the trip making such a proposal?

HAYDEN: No.

CONLEY: Mr. Hayden, who paid for your trip to North Vietnam in December, 1965?

HAYDEN: Most of the financing outside of our Free World was by the North Vietnamese, over much protest, because we would have liked to have answered the question by saying we paid for our own way, because we know the very deeply felt value that you should always pay your own way, and if somebody pays for you then you are not an independent judge.

I think I can be an independent judge no matter who pays for me. I have taken your money to fly here to talk to you, and so forth. But there is another factor. The North Vietnamese insisted that since they are in a state of war, and they were a different nation, if they were going to bring Americans into North Vietnam they would come in as guests of the government and not have to pay for the use of facilities that the government had or had access to. So, after we got through to Czechoslovakia, we did not have to pay the rest of the trip, and did not have to pay the food and lodging expenses in Hanoi.

CONLEY: Did you pay personally for the trip—

HAYDEN: I paid a round-trip to Czechoslovakia.

CONLEY: From the United States?

HAYDEN: Yes.

CONLEY: Out of your own personal funds, sir?

HAYDEN: Yes, or whatever I raised from friends. It was my money. I can check it for you and write a letter or something. The second trip to North Vietnam, by the way, I paid for altogether out of my own funds.

CONLEY: Then the North Vietnamese, as I understand you, from Czechoslovakia to North Vietnam paid your round-trip fare, is that correct?

HAYDEN: I don't believe they paid because they do not believe in money exactly the same way. The United States paid my way back.

CONLEY: The North Vietnamese government either paid or took care of your transportation from Czechoslovakia to North Vietnam and back to Czechoslovakia?

HAYDEN: Maybe back to Moscow. I think we came back from Hanoi, Peking, Moscow, New York, or something like that. This is all recorded elsewhere, sir.

CONLEY: In connection with your stay in North Vietnam were you a guest of the Vietnam Peace Committee?

HAYDEN: Well, I would say they were sort of our hosts. They were responsible for our welfare and safety because of the American bombing. They provided us with interpreters.

CONLEY: Do you know whether the Vietnamese committee has any official standing in the North Vietnamese government?

HAYDEN: No, I'm not sure exactly how they are funded. I'm sure it is some kind of government funding. I'm not sure how. I think if you read our book we have some explanation of it, but I can't recall the nature of the organization.

CONLEY: Mr. Hayden, I have asked you earlier whether you met Colonel Lau on this trip to North Vietnam in December, 1965, and you have indicated you did. Have you had occasion since that time to maintain contact with Colonel Lau?

HAYDEN: Yes, I saw Colonel Lau the second time I went to

North Vietnam, in October of last year. As I said before, I saw Colonel Lau momentarily in Paris when I was carrying out that mission that I want to explain to you and discuss.

CONLEY: Now, Mr. Hayden, I want to show you a letter.

HAYDEN: I know this letter.

CONLEY: Dated June 4, 1968. It bears the signature of Tom Hayden, does it not?

HAYDEN: Yes.

CONLEY: Is that your signature?

HAYDEN: Yes. This whole letter I will take complete credit for.

CONLEY: In other words, this letter which has been previously offered as an exhibit—

HAYDEN: It is a stolen letter. You collaborated with police agencies to take this out of somebody's briefcase. It is not a secret letter, although I object to the method by which you obtained it.*

CONLEY: You indicate that this letter which has been previously offered as an exhibit in these hearings is in fact a letter which you prepared the original of and of which I have handed you a photocopy?

HAYDEN: As far as I know.

CONLEY: Did you give the original copy of this letter to Mr. Robert Greenblatt?

HAYDEN: Yes.

CONLEY: Do you recall the day you gave it to him?

HAYDEN: No. I think that he was going to somewhere in Europe to some kind of conference. He was expecting to be able to stop on the way back through Paris because we wanted to understand what the situation was in the peace

* When Robert Greenblatt returned from Paris via Canada in June, he was searched at the border by U.S. authorities, charged with possessing drugs, and had all his papers taken. Among the papers was this letter, which somehow found its way into HUAC files.

talks that were going on. I gave him an introductory note to Colonel Lau, which I will be glad to read to you.

CONLEY: No. I think the letter has already been read into the record, Mr. Hayden. You did give this letter to Mr. Greenblatt, then, at his request?

HAYDEN: I don't remember whether it was Greenblatt's request. I may have just proposed that he should stop in Paris and try to get some information on what the state of the talks was.

CONLEY: May I have the letter back?

HAYDEN: I would like to write some things from it, since I never expected to see it again.

ICHORD: We will prepare a copy for you.

HAYDEN: I will just scribble one thing. That this should be taken at the Canadian border under a false search-and-seizure process should be known to the press in this room.

CONLEY: Mr. Hayden, in order that I understand your last answer completely, Mr. Greenblatt may have asked you for this letter or you may have been aware of the fact he was going to Paris?

HAYDEN: I don't know where he was going. He may have been going to Europe.

CONLEY: I wondered what prompted you to write a letter to Colonel Lau.

HAYDEN: Colonel Lau is one of the people that I know in the North Vietnamese delegation. I thought that it would be possible for Greenblatt to have a discussion with him and that he required an introductory note. At that time I was very enthusiastic about the situation. I was under the illusion temporarily that the war might be ending. But we wanted to know very much what the Paris talks were accomplishing and several of us were in Paris on several occasions talking to both State Department officials and North Vietnamese officials, trying to get a picture.

I have written my own picture of what was going on in Paris in *Ramparts* magazine. Anyone these days who is going to Paris from the peace movement I will be glad to give a letter to so that they can go try to see the North Vietnamese, who don't trust Americans for some reason.

ASHBROOK: Do they trust you?

HAYDEN: They trust me enough to have a conversation. I doubt, Mr. Ashbrook, that they would see you.

ASHBROOK: I doubt that I would want to see them.

HAYDEN: You would not want to see them? You would not want to talk to them?

ASHBROOK: I have no reason to.

HAYDEN: I didn't think you would. That is quite a peaceful attitude.

CONLEY: Mr. Hayden, directing your attention specifically to this letter, it is addressed to Colonel Lau, is it not? It is written to Colonel Lau?

HAYDEN: It is an introductory note for Greenblatt.

CONLEY: I specifically read to you the next-to-the-last paragraph, which says, "We hope that the current Paris discussions go well for you." This is implying, as I read the note, that you are hoping they go well for Colonel Lau, or for the North Vietnamese people. Is that not correct?

HAYDEN: Yes, it is correct. It is literally correct. I was very hopeful that at last the thing was winding up and after the agony of twenty-five years of war, which involved many fruitless attempts at negotiation, that this finally was it, people were getting together at the table and that it would be possible for the bombing to be ended and the American troops to be withdrawn from South Vietnam.

CONLEY: As I read this particular sentence it is not wishing the Vietnamese people, it is wishing a particular group within Vietnam.

HAYDEN: My views are well known on that. In a war you

can only decide one side is right and the other side is wrong. My government, which I don't think represents me, is wrong in Vietnam. There is only one other group to say it is right and that is the people of Vietnam, and the National Liberation Front in the South and the North Vietnamese government. They are right in wanting the United States out of Vietnam. We have no business in Vietnam. They're right in wanting the bombing to end, and so forth. I have always said that.

CONLEY: Are you saying that you support the North Vietnamese, then, in their efforts?

HAYDEN: I support their position. Their position is that the United States should get out of Vietnam. That is also the position of Communists, non-Communists, anti-Communists the world over. Do you support the proposition the United States should stay in? There are only two things you can stand for on this, out or in.

CONLEY: You are the witness, I am the counsel.

HAYDEN: Okay.

CONLEY: It also says here, "The news from South Vietnam seems very good indeed."

HAYDEN: It looked like the war was winding up.

CONLEY: What about the second *Tet* offensive, which was in the process of occurring at that time? Is that what you had reference to?

HAYDEN: No, the entire situation in the country was improved immensely, I thought, because of the beginning of the Paris talks, and the news from Vietnam was just good.

CONLEY: The news from South Vietnam at that particular time was the second *Tet* offensive.

HAYDEN: That was two months before the letter was written. The second *Tet* offensive was early May.

CONLEY: This was early June. I say the *Tet* offensive was just winding up.

HAYDEN: No, it was not just winding up. Actually, it never stopped, if you want to get into the reality of the defeat, the tragic defeat of the United States troops there.

CONLEY: Mr. Hayden, you conclude the letter with the closing, "good fortune, victory."

HAYDEN: Right.

CONLEY: What do you mean by the words "good fortune?"

HAYDEN: I hope it is all over, I hope peace can be restored at last. This country has been massacred by so many countries for so many years that it just made me terribly happy to think that at last the possibility of peace in Vietnam was being a real possibility. I wished them every luck in the world. I think we owe them tremendous respect for the struggle they have endured at the hands of politicians in Washington, particularly President Johnson, and that is the meaning of the statement. I hope they win their independence and hope they keep it. I think they should be an independent country. Whether Communist or not, it is their business, not Rusk's or President Johnson's.

CONLEY: You did not send it to the Vietnamese people. You sent it to a particular officer within a particular segment of the country of Vietnam.

HAYDEN: To me the Vietnamese people, insofar as they are organized, are organized in a united way against the United States. The other Vietnamese are fictional characters invented to make us believe at home that we are somehow supporting the government there. But we are not supporting the government there. It would fall in a minute of its own corruption if it were not for the United States military. It is like saying in the American Revolution, the American people were the American revolutionaries. Surely there were some Americans working for the British, just as there were Vietnamese working for the French, and now working for the Americans. But when you said "the Americans" versus "the British" there was no question you were talking about the American revolutionaries.

CONLEY: Are you saying the North Vietnamese are the only government you recognize yourself as existing in Vietnam?

HAYDEN: No. The North Vietnamese government, by virtue of the fact that the Geneva Agreements were never implemented, is a de facto government north of the Seventeenth Parallel. South of the Seventeenth Parallel the de facto government, in my opinion as an objective observer, as much as I can be, the only real government in South Vietnam is the National Liberation Front. The Americans admit that when they say that their whole zone of South Vietnam has been under Viet Cong control for the last twenty years.

We forget that the Vietnamese succeeded in liberating all of Vietnam from the French in 1945. Ho Chi Minh's administration stretched to the south down to the Ca Mau Peninsula. The attempt by the French, and now the Americans ever since, has been to kind of roll back that revolutionary victory, roll back that nationalist revolution. It still remains in South Vietnam. The Viet Minh, who now are the Viet Cong, are still there and they function, they collect taxes, they have an army, they have schools, they have hospitals, they have all of the things which you and I would say governments have.

WATSON: May I ask at this point in order to establish your objectivity, have you visited South Vietnam?

HAYDEN: No, I would like to very much but I am sure I would be killed.

WATSON: Have you visited South Vietnam?

HAYDEN: I cannot, because it is too dangerous with the Americans there, to visit if you have been in Hanoi.

WATSON: I could appreciate that fact but I just wanted—

HAYDEN: I am sure you could.

WATSON: I was trying to ascertain your objectivity in assessing the various governments.

CONLEY: Mr. Hayden, one other question: The letter concludes with the word "victory." Am I to imply from that that you are wishing victory to Colonel Lau and his people?

HAYDEN: No. When I say victory I mean that the end of the war in Vietnam and the withdrawal of the American troops would be the greatest victory possible for the people of this country and for the people of Vietnam, including Colonel Lau, a victory over the people like Rusk and Johnson and other old men who have been dominating foreign policy with wacko conceptions of communism for the last twenty years, a victory over the draft boards in the United States, whose average age is fifty-eight years old.

ASHBROOK: Particularly over the American servicemen there?

HAYDEN: No, we are the closest friends the American servicemen have, I think. We want them out of Vietnam. We are not the reason that they are being killed.

We are finding that it is more and more possible to organize within the armed forces and around Army bases. We believe that the GIs in Vietnam are increasingly against the war and think that they are merely cannon fodder for Washington while elections are settled and prestige is traded around.

WATSON: In fact, Mr. Hayden, you are encouraging direct action on the part of military men of America to go AWOL and refuse to serve in Vietnam?

HAYDEN: What is your evidence for that, Mr. Watson?

WATSON: So far as your special publications of SDS and other newspapers are directed at servicemen—You are aware of that activity, aren't you?

HAYDEN: I'm aware of the activity.

WATSON: That is all I want to know, thank you.

HAYDEN: What does that have to do with what I think should be done? I would like to explain to you what I think of servicemen. I respect those who have deserted. I think it is a very brave thing. I think it would be better, if possible, to stay in the armed forces, not shoot any Vietnamese, and come home alive. I think a lot of them will. I think the revolt is

132

going on clearly by soldiers in South Vietnam against their commanding officers and especially against Johnson.

ICHORD: On what do you base that?

HAYDEN: Riots in the prison camps, widespread interviews published in various magazines, letters I have seen from GIs who are fed up with this war. They don't like peaceniks because they think we are not fighters and we are taking an easy way out. That is their business, that is their opinion, but I identify with them. I think young men like myself are over there and I think there has to be good relations in the future between those young American men who fought in Vietnam and those young American men who oppose the war in Vietnam, and that is what we are working towards.

I think that the reason, the very fundamental reason, if you inquire in your committees and in your secret investigations, the reason the war is getting harder and harder to fight is that the American GIs cannot be pushed out there to continue fighting, because they don't think it is worth it. That is a factor that a general has to take into account.

ASHBROOK: Do you think you are talking for 500,000 servicemen?

HAYDEN: It is just becoming clear that servicemen over there don't want to fight this war.

ASHBROOK: What numbers indicate that?

HAYDEN: I don't know what numbers. What numbers do you think, Mr. Ashbrook?

ASHBROOK: I don't agree with you. It is your allegation. You say increasing numbers of servicemen, and pretty soon you are talking about all servicemen. Roughly there are 500,000 servicemen there. How many do you think will identify with what you are saying?

HAYDEN: I think most servicemen would not identify with me or my position, but would identify with the idea that this war stinks and that they should be home and if Johnson wants to go to Vietnam or you want to go to Vietnam, you Congressmen, to fight, that is all well and good but that is not the place for young Americans.

ICHORD: Mr. Hayden, I was in South Vietnam in June, 1967, and talked to well over a thousand enlisted men individually.

HAYDEN: Talked to a thousand enlisted individually?

ICHORD: Talked to a thousand enlisted men individually. My impression was that their morale was surprisingly high.

HAYDEN: I'm afraid you were brainwashed.

ICHORD: By the enlisted men?

HAYDEN: By the people who organized your trip. Probably the generals that Governor Romney spoke about.

ICHORD: I will state to you that the enlisted men whom I interviewed on an individual basis, and in groups of fifty or sixty, were not picked by anybody. I picked them myself. But that is a matter of assessment. You haven't been there—

HAYDEN: Did you talk to veterans of Khe Sanh?

ICHORD: As a matter of fact, I was in Khe Sanh.

HAYDEN: While it was the chief thing that we had to hold forever, or while it was something we had to evacuate?

ICHORD: Of course the siege of Khe Sanh had not occurred. That occurred subsequent to June, 1967. But we have gone far afield here.

WATSON: Mr. Chairman, if I may say one further word. Mr. Hayden is correct, although earlier he didn't seem to know too much about this publication directed toward the military urging them to desert and so forth; apparently now you do recall something about it. But they run periodically some letters in this publication, most of them anonymous letters, allegedly from veterans of Vietnam or people in Vietnam who are against war.

HAYDEN: I have letters.

WATSON: No doubt he has some letters.

134

HAYDEN: I would like to discuss what I did in Paris. It is curious to me I haven't been asked.

ICHORD: We are going to get to Paris.

CONLEY: We will get to Paris. Mr. Hayden, I cannot help but note that you have again, for the fourth time as I count it, given a different meaning to the word "victory," as you have with the words "guerrilla," "militant," and "attack." Perhaps it is just a question of semantics between you and me that we are unable to define these words or give the same meaning to them.

HAYDEN: What about deeds? Lets try deeds.

CONLEY: I don't recall your using the word "deeds."

HAYDEN: If you can't understand my words I would like to know what it is about my actions that you have in mind? What have I attacked?

CONLEY: I said there were three words that we have had trouble with today, the word "guerrilla," the word "militant," and the word "attack." Perhaps you did not hear what I said.

HAYDEN: What was the trouble? I explained what I meant by the words.

CONLEY: Yes, and your explanation would not, I think, be the common, sensible explanation for the meaning of those particular words any more than your explanation for the word "victory," meaning bringing the soldiers home.

DI SUVARO: Could we go on, Mr. Chairman, because I think the counsel is being argumentative.

ICHORD: Just a minute. We are following the rules pretty well thus far. We are dealing in semantics here.

HAYDEN: We are also dealing with things I have written in dozens of places. It is unnecessary to go over them here as far as I can see.

ICHORD: Certainly, Mr. Hayden, I would say these words that you have written will have meaning to some people. It apparently has a different meaning to you than the ordinary connotation that I would accept as the meaning. That is one of the reasons for the question.

ASHBROOK: Not only that but also the word "pinned." I think everybody has some common understanding of what is meant when you are going to pin delegates in a convention. The other word is, "anything to stop this farce," and of course to him "anything" would not mean what it would normally mean to others. The word "guerrilla," "attack," and "victory"—

HAYDEN: Before the joking goes further, aren't you embarrassed and discomfited by the existence of this gigantic [Walker] report which goes over in much greater detail than you could, because you don't have the funds, thank God, or the staff to do it; everything, I mean, meetings, all the things that you have been asking about are listed in here. These investigators didn't have too much difficulty understanding what our position was, what we were planning to do, what our applications for permits meant, what happened in meetings. Maybe because you don't have the staff or the machinery to collect the information that these people collected, but they have not raised the questions that you are raising about whether—

ASHBROOK: Maybe this is why we are raising them.

HAYDEN: So you are not embarrassed by this, but you sort of disagree with its conclusions or analysis?

CONLEY: I think we need to make it clear that that document to which you refer carries neither the approval or disapproval of that particular commission, but is merely one of three task reports.

HAYDEN: Beautiful. That is what I said, though.

ICHORD: We should make it clear it is a staff report.

HAYDEN: I said it was done by an authorized task force three or four times earlier today.

ASHBROOK: Which has neither been accepted or rejected by the committee.

HAYDEN: Is that your last refuge? Obviously, it is not going to be accepted by the committee, Milton Eisenhower and those people, but they have been done in by their own staff. Their own staff went out and looked at the situation and could not come to any conclusions other than the ones they came to.

ICHORD: The committee will have the opportunity to read the staff report.

CONLEY: Mr. Hayden, if I may belabor you one moment further on this particular letter that you wrote for Mr. Greenblatt, I notice in here the last sentence in the first paragraph, "He works closely with myself and with Dave Dellinger and has just returned from Hanoi." What was the significance of mentioning that Mr. Greenblatt works closely with yourself and with Dave Dellinger?

HAYDEN: I wanted to identify this person as a person who is active in the Mobilization, and the way to do that would be to identify him with two people, myself and Dave Dellinger, who visited North Vietnam and who are known to the North Vietnamese.

CONLEY: Both you and Mr. Dellinger had previously met with Colonel Lau, had you not?

HAYDEN: You mean together?

CONLEY: Not together, but you have both met Colonel Lau, have you not?

HAYDEN: Yes. I said I have met him, and Dave Dellinger is a member of the Tribunal that found the United States guilty of genocide. Colonel Lau was the North Vietnamese person in charge of marshaling the evidence for the North Vietnamese case. So he would know Colonel Lau through the examination of mutilated and napalmed Vietnamese bodies.

CONLEY: If we may move back to one other question that came up earlier, you were asked, I believe, whether you were aware of the fact whether *Rat* was or was not a publication of SDS.

137

HAYDEN: I said it was not.

CONLEY: I do call to your attention the fact that in the publication *Vocations for Social Change*—Are you aware of this publication?

HAYDEN: Haywood, California?

CONLEY: Yes, sir. The October, 1968, issue advises people who want a job with *Rat* to apply as follows—

HAYDEN: "The *Rat,* care of SDS, 131 Prince Street, New York, New York."

It gives the phone number, contact Jeff Shero. That could mean anything, but what it does not mean is that the *Rat* is a SDS publication. SDS, 131 Prince Street, could be a New York chapter of SDS. I don't know what it is. It may be a temporary office of the *Rat,* it may not. But it is not an official SDS publication.

The SDS publication is *New Left Notes.* But Jeffrey Shero is a former officer of some kind of SDS, I mean some kind in SDS, and he is the editor and founder of the *Rat.* A lot of SDS people are active in New York City, just as there are other Movement groups in New York City and they all identify very closely with the *Rat.* But the *Rat* is an independent publication published by these five or six people as far as I know.

CONLEY: Mr. Hayden, in September, 1967, did you attend a meeting in Bratislava, Czechoslovakia, with representatives of the Viet Cong and North Vietnamese?

HAYDEN: Yes. That is another thing that is available.

CONLEY: Mr. Hayden, in a document sent out under the signature of Dave Dellinger, appears the following quotation: "The Prague conference is intended to create solidarity and mutual understanding between the revolutionaries from Vietnam and their American supporters who are trying to change the United States."

Mr. Hayden, my question to you, sir, would be, Did you receive a copy of this particular document? Have you seen it before today?

138

HAYDEN: I must have seen it. I had a hand in preparing this document. I was one of the people who helped to write the agenda and work out an agenda for the conference. What you read from is a true statement of one of the purposes of the conference.

CONLEY: Mr. Hayden, let me ask you this question, if I may, sir, with reference to that statement. Are you, sir, one of the American supporters of the revolutionaries mentioned there in Vietnam?

HAYDEN: I have already said I am.

CONLEY: Thank you, sir.

HAYDEN: Very few people in the world are not.

CONLEY: Mr. Hayden, while you were in Czechoslovakia at this conference in September of 1967, were you asked by the Viet Cong representatives to go to the capital of Cambodia to receive three American war prisoners?

HAYDEN: Well, this is a very delicate area. I'm glad to get into it but I will have to listen to your questions very carefully. So if you will restate that.

CONLEY: I will read it again to you.

While you were in Czechoslovakia did the Viet Cong representatives ask you to go to the capital of Cambodia to take custody of three American prisoners of war?

HAYDEN: Not exactly. I, as you know, have been involved in the release of American prisoners on three occasions—well, several occasions—and totaling altogether three American prisoners from South Vietnam and six American pilots from North Vietnam, all of whom are here in the United States now.

The way in which these releases were effected is very complicated and delicate. I will be very happy to speak as frankly as I can about it but I want us to be very careful because the implication that you are making that somehow the linkups between the peace movement, people like myself and Hanoi, is bad, is the kind of thing that is going to go out around the

139

world as an item of news and it is going to appear, whether you like it or not, it is going to appear as sort of an official United States government committee condemning these operations which have resulted in the release of prisoners. And I am very concerned about the welfare of those prisoners—not that I think the Vietnamese would do anything to them—but the possibility of any American being released is always useful, helpful, and basically good. So we have to discuss it in a way that respects the situation.

CONLEY: Mr. Hayden, I think you read more malice in my question than I intended.

HAYDEN: I was trying to set the groundwork.

CONLEY: My question was simple: Were you asked to go to the capital of Cambodia? I am not asking you to go into a detailed explanation of anything.

HAYDEN: The literal answer to your literal question is no.

CONLEY: Thank you, sir. Now, then, in connection with that same general proposition, did you not, in fact, in November, 1967, go to Hanoi and from there to the capital of Cambodia where you took custody of three United States sergeants who had been held as prisoners of war?

HAYDEN: Incorrect, again.

CONLEY: Would you like to explain?

HAYDEN: I would prefer not to explain more than I have explained in many publications and statements. I was involved in the release of these prisoners. It did not quite exactly happen according to the geographic route you described.

CONLEY: Are you quarreling with going from Hanoi to Cambodia? Is that it?

HAYDEN: That and going from Czechoslovakia to Cambodia, and so forth.

CONLEY: I never suggested you went from Czechoslovakia to Cambodia.

HAYDEN: I thought the first question was, did I go from that conference to Cambodia?

CONLEY: No, sir. My question was, were you approached at the conference in Czechoslovakia and asked if you would go to the capital of Cambodia?

HAYDEN: No.

ASHBROOK: May I change that question, because as I recall his answer, he said "literally" that was not correct. Was the conference at Czechoslovakia the place at which you learned that you could take custody of the servicemen if you were to be in Cambodia?

HAYDEN: Not exactly. There had been discussions ever since our first trip to Vietnam about the worries that American families have about prisoners there. We had always stressed that while we did not feel that the North Vietnamese had any legal or other kind of responsibility to release the prisoners, we thought it would be a highly humane and important act that could contribute to making peace easier to negotiate.

ASHBROOK: Not for propaganda purposes?

HAYDEN: Propaganda works both ways. Every time the Vietnamese have released prisoners, the United States releases prisoners, and announces it although the actions are not reciprocal, neither side does not recognize that the other has done it, and so forth.

It was at this conference in Bratislava during the discussions with the Vietnamese about the state of American prisoners that some Vietnamese approached myself and said that they were contemplating the possible release of some prisoners from South Vietnam. They were not sure how to do it technically. They had a lot of problems. Contrary to public opinion, people do not run up and down from North to South Vietnam on the Ho Chi Minh trail. These prisoners were deep in South Vietnam.

141

A way had to be found for them to be released without the National Liberation Front having to hand them directly over to the Americans because they did not recognize each other. The problem was never solved in the first discussions but I said that I was ready at any point to participate in such a release if I could be of value and service. Some time later, not too much later, I think a month or month and a half, the word did come that such a thing was possible. I happened to be in Paris at the time and at that time I went to Cambodia to work out the arrangements.

CONLEY: You did not then go to Hanoi and from there to Cambodia?

HAYDEN: I went to Hanoi but not particularly related to prisoners. I went to Hanoi to see what two years of bombing had done in the way of destruction.

CONLEY: Did you go to Hanoi prior to going to Cambodia?

HAYDEN: I went to Cambodia and to Hanoi and back to Cambodia because that is the way you go, and then to France and back to Cambodia and back to New York. It was not all related.

CONLEY: Had you been to Hanoi before you went to Cambodia and took custody of these three prisoners?

HAYDEN: I had been to Hanoi twice by then. The prisoners were from South Vietnam, not related to North Vietnam.

ICHORD: Were they held by North Vietnamese?

HAYDEN: No, NLF.

CONLEY: Mr. Hayden, directing your attention to January of this year, did you make a trip to Havana, Cuba?

HAYDEN: Yes.

CONLEY: To take part in the International Cultural Congress, which was a gathering of Communists and other revolutionaries whose aim is to destroy the non-Communist governments of the world?

HAYDEN: I don't remember those aims being enunciated in quite that way. But then there are no more people like yourself in Cuba. It was essentially a meeting of intellectuals who are not strong enough to pick up a gun and were film makers, painters.

CONLEY: Do I have the title right, the International Cultural Congress?

HAYDEN: It was a cultural congress in Havana. I don't know if it was called the International Cultural Congress.

WATSON: Mr. Counsel, the witness is not implying that there are not some intellectuals who are fighting for this country? You are not implying that, are you?

HAYDEN: Oh, no.

WATSON: You said earlier that they were not strong enough to lift a gun.

HAYDEN: I was replying to the suggestion that this was a meeting of armed revolutionaries which was implied although not exactly stated by the question. I wanted to indicate that it was a meeting of intellectuals.

WATSON: Do you consider yourself an intellectual?

HAYDEN: I never thought about it.

CONLEY: Mr. Hayden, how long were you in Cuba attending this conference?

HAYDEN: About ten days to fifteen days.

CONLEY: Would you describe briefly, if you can, exactly what you did at the conference?

HAYDEN: Nothing.

CONLEY: I did not mean you as an individual. I mean what was done at the conference? Was it a discussion?

HAYDEN: Yes.

CONLEY: Discussion group.

ICHORD: Would you say it was not a very productive conference?

HAYDEN: I got a lot of things I wanted to get. I talked to a lot of people. I wanted to see what Cuba was like. But I went as a journalist through a strange deal with the Department of State, who would not allow me a passport to go as a delegate.

So I didn't participate, I didn't have any official status in the conference, I did not speak, I did not operate as a delegate.*

Around the site of the conference I was able to meet and talk with people from Latin America, the Middle East, Western Europe. There were Vietnamese people there. I just took advantage of the occasion to talk to as many people as I could.

CONLEY: Mr. Hayden, is it a fair statement to say that the congress closed with an appeal to the intellectuals to boycott United States academic and cultural programs?

HAYDEN: There was such an appeal. It had more to it than that.

CONLEY: You participated—

HAYDEN: I did not participate in the drafting of the appeal although I agree with the appeal.

CONLEY: What particular publication did you represent at this conference?

HAYDEN: I just went as a writer. I didn't have to represent a publication.

CONLEY: I thought you indicated that you did, though, sir.

HAYDEN: No.

CONLEY: Perhaps I misunderstood you.

HAYDEN: No. I can check it in my documents but I think I just agreed not to go as a delegate.

CONLEY: You did not represent any particular newspaper or magazine then?

HAYDEN: I think I may have gone as an editor or associate editor of *Liberation,* which is a pacifist magazine edited by

* The following exchange over whether I "participated" in the Havana congress might seem irrelevant to the reader. The reason Conley pursued the question, I believe, was to discover if I violated the terms of my passport to Cuba. In order to get State Department validation for the Cuba trip, I signed affidavits testifying that my purpose was journalism rather than politics. Therefore, if I testified before HUAC that I participated, my passport might be subject to invalidation.

Dave Dellinger, with which I had ties for a while, but I haven't been active with them for some time.

CONLEY: When was the last time you were active with *Liberation* magazine?

HAYDEN: I never was very active. That is why I decided to not have my name on the masthead.

CONLEY: Was any of the material related to the Havana conference published in the *Liberation* magazine?

HAYDEN: It was published by Dellinger.

CONLEY: Written by you, sir?

HAYDEN: No. I certainly had talks with Dellinger relating to the article he finally wrote.

       ✻   ✻   ✻

CONLEY: Directing your attention specifically to a news item which appeared in the *National Guardian* of December 30, 1968, under the byline of Lionel Martin:

"Those who to date have stressed their intention to participate in the congress from the United States are antiwar activists Dave Dellinger, Tom Hayden, community organizer in Newark, New Jersey, and Conor Cruise O'Brien, Professor of Humanities at New York University. Many others are expected to attend from the United States."

This article would indicate that you were attending as a participant. In fact, I believe it uses that word.

HAYDEN: I am sorry. Did you ask a question?

CONLEY: Yes, sir.

HAYDEN: I thought you just made a statement.

CONLEY: My question was, sir, that the article says that you attended as a participant. Is this correct?

HAYDEN: Well, you didn't even read the article, then.

CONLEY: I am reading to you the paragraph that deals specifically with you, going to that conference.

HAYDEN: But your own testimony here, sir, is that I went to the Congress in January, and the article is dated December 30.

CONLEY: This article was obviously written prior to the— read the paragraph that I have reference to, sir.

HAYDEN: Well, it is an article that says what you said, but—

ICHORD: Mr. Counsel, instead of asking the witness about what the article says, ask him—

HAYDEN: Are you saying that it does say that?

ICHORD: Ask him whether or not he was a participant.

HAYDEN: We already testified that.

CONLEY: This article, Mr. Hayden, was written prior to the conference.

HAYDEN: So what?

CONLEY: Is Mr. Martin mistaken, or did he make a false statement in that article, to say that you were going to be a participant?

HAYDEN: That is between you and Mr. Martin.

ICHORD: The witness is saying that he testified that he was not a participant?

HAYDEN: I testified, in fact; you know what I testified.

CONLEY: Yes, sir, you have testified that you did not participate?

HAYDEN: Of course.

CONLEY: But this article, let me read it again to you, sir.

HAYDEN: You didn't read it.

CONLEY: "Those who to date have expressed their intention to participate in the Congress from the United States are as follows."

HAYDEN: So what?

CONLEY: All right. Now the word "participate," perhaps we are getting hung up again on what words mean.

HAYDEN: Perhaps you are, my friend, but I don't believe everything I read in the newspapers. It is a matter of record that I did not participate as a delegate in that Congress.

146

CONLEY: Then, sir, my question—

HAYDEN: It is a matter of record, as I said yesterday, that I went in my capacity as an editor of *Liberation* magazine, but the main problem is I don't understand what you are uptight about.

ICHORD: The record will stand as made, Mr. Counsel. Proceed with the next question.

CONLEY: The next question is—

ICHORD: I don't always agree, or believe what I read in the newspapers.

CONLEY: The next question, then, is that Mr. Martin is mistaken?

HAYDEN: That is between you and Mr. Martin. You have my testimony.

CONLEY: I am asking you, sir, is this article correct, as far as it pertains—

HAYDEN: You have my testimony.

ICHORD: We have his testimony, Mr. Counsel. Proceed to the next question.

HAYDEN: It is ridiculous.

CONLEY: All right, now directing your attention to another article in the *National Guardian,* dated January 27, 1968, and written again by Mr. Lionel Martin, *Guardian* staff correspondent, bylined Havana: "Participants"—and I am reading from the paragraph, the first paragraph to introduce the article says, "The International Cultural Congress closed here with an appeal to intellectuals to boycott U.S. academic and cultural programs."

Moving down in the article, there is a subheadline which says, "Participants from U.S."

"The Congress was attended by some 500 delegates and observers from 70 countries and more than 100 journalists. Participating from the U.S. were antiwar leader Dave Dellinger, community organizer Tom Hayden, moviemakers Dick

Moore and Saul Landau, cartoonist Jules Feiffer," and on and on and on.

Again, the editor or the reporter, after the conference, says that you participated in the conference.

HAYDEN: So what? I have testified that I did not.

CONLEY: And I am asking you, sir, I put to you the question now—

HAYDEN: Put it.

CONLEY: —is this reporter in error when he says that you participated?

HAYDEN: Yes, he is in error.

CONLEY: Thank you, sir. And he is a reporter for the *National Guardian?*

HAYDEN: That is the first time I ever heard you fellows believe the *National Guardian*. I can even give you my press badge, for one of your exhibits. That was made in Cuba, and it might not be valid to bring it into the United States.

CONLEY: Mr. Hayden, directing your attention to another subject, some time ago, Capt. Charles Kinney, of the Newark Police Department, testified before this committee—

HAYDEN: Yes.

CONLEY: Would you like to say something else?

HAYDEN: No, no, go ahead.

CONLEY: —testified before this committee in connection with the riots which occurred in Newark in the summer of 1967, and during the testimony of Captain Kinney, with reference to these particular riots, he quoted from an article which appeared in the *New York Times,* under date of December 15, 1967, in which you are quoted as follows: "A case can be made for violence in the peace movement. It is not as if violence in the slums and in Vietnam appear in a vacuum. It came only after the failure of democratic methods. When I participate in violence, it was out of that failing, not as an expression of psychological self-hatred."

148

Mr. Hayden, would you please advise us as to what circumstances you are willing to participate in violence?

HAYDEN: Advise you?

CONLEY: Yes.

HAYDEN: Well, I have already testified about that question as it pertains to the subject of these hearings, and I went on at considerable length, trying to educate you yesterday, as to my beliefs in that area, and I think it would be redundant to go over them.

CONLEY: Sir, I am reading particularly again from this account, which is attributed to you.

"When I participate in violence, it was out of that failing, not as an expression of psychological self-hatred."

Now, when I read that quotation, and perhaps I am putting the wrong emphasis on it, you are implying that you have participated in violence, and I am asking you under what conditions do you participate in violence?

ICHORD: Mr. Counsel, I think perhaps you should lay the proper foundation, and first ask the witness whether he made that statement or not.

HAYDEN: What is the quotation from? Every quotation that you gave me yesterday you read out of context, so I would like to have the full quotation that you are now reading.

Where is the full statement? What is the date of it?

CONLEY: December 15. I don't have the clipping here.

HAYDEN: Of what year?

CONLEY: 1967.

HAYDEN: Well, I certainly would answer at a later time, but given your way of handling quotations yesterday, when I had a chance to look at the full quotation, and given the fact that I had to read into the record extensively the context of statements that you had lifted, I would not now want to comment on something that you attribute to me, because I am sure that in part it is taken out of context.

Furthermore, I have discussed violence *ad nauseam* before this committee, in reference to almost every subject that you are supposedly considering under your very vague mandate.

CONLEY: Mr. Chairman, I believe we have asked that question, and he said he would have to see the article. I do not have the article here.

ICHORD: Well, did you make—was that a correct quotation, Mr. Hayden?

HAYDEN: No, not as far as I know.

ICHORD: Do you remember making a statement to that particular reporter?

HAYDEN: I don't remember making a statement to the *New York Times* in December of 1967, though it is conceivable that I did.

CONLEY: Mr. Hayden, moving on to another subject, and one with which I am sure you are quite familiar, your book, *Rebellion in Newark*, are you familiar with that book, sir?

HAYDEN: More familiar than you.

CONLEY: I am sure that you are, sir, and I want to direct your attention specifically to pages 70–71 of that book.

HAYDEN: Could I have a copy of the book?

CONLEY: Yes, sir. Wherein appears the following, starting on page 70:

The role of organized violence is now being carefully considered. During the riot, for instance, a conscious guerrilla can participate in pulling police away from the path of people engaged in attacking stores. He can create new disorder, in new areas the police think are secure. He can carry the torch, if not to all the people, to white neighborhoods and downtown business districts. If necessary, he can successfully shoot to kill.

And the quotation continues. That is not the end of the quotation. Now, Mr. Hayden, with reference to that particular quotation that appears in that book, is that not similar to the recommendations that you made in your position papers before the Chicago demonstrations, urging that white revolutionaries organize diversionary activities to pull the police out of the black areas during the rioting, looting, and burning? Do you recall the testimony yesterday, sir?

HAYDEN: Yes.

CONLEY: Now is this not a similar position?

HAYDEN: No.

CONLEY: Would you explain the difference, please?

HAYDEN: Yes, the difference is that I am discussing here on page 70 what possibly is being considered, or possibly might be carried out by black people in the ghettos. In the quotation that you spoke about yesterday, I was not referring particularly to black people.

CONLEY: Is this the only distinction that you make as between the fact that in one instance, it involves black people going from the ghetto to the white neighborhoods, and in the other situation, white people rising up in the white neighborhoods?

HAYDEN: Well, if you imply that from the statement that you read yesterday that that statement implies that people are going to pull police away from the path of people engaged in attacking stores, that is unlikely, since I talked about the suburbs, which are nowhere near these stores. "Creating disorder in new areas, carrying the torch, shooting to kill." I tried to make clear yesterday what I meant by diversionary demonstrations, and it is quite different from what I say here.

ASHBROOK: You have a different meaning for everything that is said.

HAYDEN: Well, you are struggling because you can't get anything on me, and you keep hoping that there is something, a sinister meaning, but the words only mean one thing.

"The role of organized violence is now being carefully considered." Clear?

ASHBROOK: Clear.

ICHORD: I don't understand—

HAYDEN: What ambiguous meaning is there, then?

ICHORD: Let there be order.

ASHBROOK: I was waiting for your—

ICHORD: Gentlemen, let us get back on the track. I don't quite understand, Mr. Hayden, your explanation.

HAYDEN: Well, read it.

ICHORD: You say you are not advocating shoot to kill, but you set this up as a possibility of a solution? Is that your distinction?

HAYDEN: Sir?

ICHORD: They are your words.

HAYDEN: Well, there is a kind of a brainless way of analyzing going on here, or there is an attempt to find something that is not there. This is a book that analyzes what will follow from the series of rebellions in ghettos that occurred from 1964 to 1968, and if necessary, I will read into the record the entire last chapter.

ICHORD: We can have the entire chapter placed in the record.

HAYDEN: All right, then please place it there. In the meantime, I would like to read to you the full last two pages.

The role of organized violence is now being carefully considered. During a riot, for instance, a conscious guerrilla can participate in pulling police away from the path of people engaged in attacking stores. He can create disorder in new areas the police think are secure. He can carry the torch if not to all the people to white neighborhoods and downtown business districts. If necessary, he can successfully shoot to kill. The guerrilla can employ violence effectively during times of apparent peace, too. He can attack in the suburbs or slums, with paint or bullets, symbols of racial oppression. He can get away with it. If he can force the oppressive power to be passive and defensive at the point where it is administered, by the case worker, landlord, store owner, or policeman, he can build people's confidence in their ability to demand change. Persistent, accurately aimed attacks which need not be on human life to be effective might disrupt the administration of the ghetto to a crisis point where a new system would have to be considered. These tactics of disorder will be defined by the authorities as criminal anarchy, but it may be that disruption will create possibilities of meaningful change. This depends on whether the leaders of ghetto struggles can be more successful in building strong organization than they have been so far. Violence can contribute to shattering the status quo, but only politics and organization can transform it. The ghetto still needs the power to decide its destiny on such matters as urban renewal and housing, social services, policing, and taxation. Tenants still need concrete rights against landlords in public and private housing or a new system of tenant-controlled living conditions. Welfare clients still need a livable income. Consumers still need to control the quality of merchandise and service in stores where they shop. Citizens still need effective control over those who police their community. The political structures belonging to the community are needed to bargain for and maintain control over funds from government or private sources.

In order to build a more decent community, while resisting racist power, more than violence is required. People need to create self-government. We are at a point where democracy, the idea and practice of people controlling their lives, is a revolutionary issue in the United States.

Now I think that that is a clear statement. It is my own view, as much today as it was when I wrote the book. I think that what has happened in American ghettos since the book was written indicates that the book was accurate in predicting what would happen. If you look at any daily paper, you see that violence is breaking out in the urban areas, wherever people have no organized opportunities for democratic participation in resolving their problems, period.

And I think that under those conditions, violence is often times defensible.

That is absolutely separate, as I have said many times, here and other places, from the situation in Chicago. Chicago demonstrators were from out of town. They were not living in oppressive ghetto situations. They were coming into town for two, three, or perhaps four days to conduct a demonstration, and the purpose of that demonstration was to be political.

The attempt to link the statements made in a book on ghetto rebellions with what happened in Chicago misses an awful lot of the differences between a demonstration and a rebellion by people living in their own community, differences between the situation of black people in the United States and the situation of white students, and so on and so forth.

Now what is there left to say? I will be glad to repeat again what I just said. I think I said it yesterday. I am on public record as having said it other times, and other places, and again, I feel that the discussion is becoming redundant.

ICHORD: The record will stand as made.

CONLEY: Mr. Hayden, my specific question is now that you have the book in front of you and the particular paragraph on page 70, I hand you back what has previously been marked as an exhibit before this committee, which is your "Movement Campaign 1968."

I invite your attention to page 15, under the subtitle "Black Rebellions," and my question is still what it was some minutes ago: Is there not a striking similarity between what is expressed in the book on page 70 and what is expressed on page 15 of that particular handbook for the Convention?

HAYDEN: No, there is not, again—

CONLEY: Would you be kind enough—

HAYDEN: I believe increasingly that it is impossible to educate you, or to speak with you, and this will be the last time, and then we will move to another kind of discussion. This will be the last time.

I said yesterday, both in general and through examples, what was meant by this statement, and I will say it now in another way. After the outbreak of rebellions in more than a hundred cities, after the assassination of Martin Luther King this spring I helped to organize a meeting in Washington of white people from around the country who are increasingly concerned with how to work within the white community directly against racism.

These are people from Detroit, from Boston, from New Jersey, places where rebellions had occurred, either the previous year or that year, and we discussed the variety of things that could be done, and the main things that we felt could be done were essentially political things.

For example, when the Roxbury riots seemed to be precipitated this spring, the Boston people organized in a group called "People Against Racism," organized a rally in downtown Boston, prior to the eruption and expanding, in which they called for no troops being brought in, and 20,000 people attended the rally, and I believe that being able to bring that number of white people into the downtown area of the city got them out of their usual fear which keeps them at home when they think there is going to be racial trouble.

It had a political impact on the mayor of the city, whose observers were there, and I think he himself attended, and I think that it had an effect in cooling that situation.

And I gave a number of other examples, but at no time did I advocate or carry into practice the shooting or disruptions or whatever—

CONLEY: Mr. Hayden, I haven't asked you that question. I think you are belaboring the issue.

HAYDEN: Well, I know you better than you know you, then, because I know what you are after. I am just trying to get it out on the table, and as long as you haven't asked me it, then we can put it off the table, but then don't imply it. Don't bring it up, I don't want to hear anything about it; it is out of order.

CONLEY: Let us answer the question. The question is—

HAYDEN: No, they are not similar.

CONLEY: Could you be kind enough—

HAYDEN: I will not be kind enough to tell you why they are not similar, no.

CONLEY: In other words, you would prefer to make a speech.

HAYDEN: I would prefer to forget any attempt to be civil, or have a dialogue with you, at this point. Because I have been here for six, seven, eight hours. No witness in the history of your silly committee has ever granted you a fuller statement of his philosophy, or his views, or allowed himself to be subjected to more insane questioning, without taking offense to it, without complaining about it, and now I am going to begin, because I am tired of you—

ICHORD: Let the questions be put.

HAYDEN: —pulling out of your folder—

ICHORD: The Chair will decide on whether the questions shall be admissible.

HAYDEN: —newspapers published, asking me if what is said in those newspapers is true—

ICHORD: Let there be order here.

HAYDEN: There is no order. That is what I am getting at, Mr. Chairman.

ASHBROOK: So long as we are straightening up the record, and you say I never urged that, is the committee also to understand that *U.S. News and World Report* of September 9, 1968, is wrong?

HAYDEN: You know it is wrong.

ASHBROOK: No, I don't know it is wrong; I am asking you, in your statement that you said in addressing a rally in Grant Park, and I quote, "That they want blood to flow from our heads, but blood will flow from a lot of other heads around this city and around this country. We must take to the streets, for the streets belong to the people. It may well be that the era"—

HAYDEN: Sir, I have already stated, over and over, what I feel about that.

ASHBROOK: Now wait a minute. Let me finish.

ICHORD: I don't think this question has been asked.

ASHBROOK: "It may well be that the era of organized peaceful and orderly demonstrations is coming to an end, and that other methods will be needed."

This is attributed to you. I say "attributed," as a direct quote, in a *U.S. News and World Report* of September 9, now following up on your statement, which you just made, that you never at any time urged that, this type of action, did you say this, or is the *U.S. News and World Report* story wrong?

HAYDEN: You see, there is a kind of a—there is, maybe there is a brainlessness here.

ASHBROOK: I don't have any trouble understanding it.

HAYDEN: You do have trouble. You do have trouble understanding it.

ASHBROOK: I have no trouble—

ICHORD: I think the question is very pertinent. Is this a misquotation of your statement?

HAYDEN: No, it is what I have been virtually saying in exactly the same words for two days before you.

That if you are attacked by somebody, and your head is split, that I believe that it is within your legislative rights to, at least moral rights, to hit back.

ASHBROOK: That is a very—

HAYDEN: That is very different from what we have just got done reading, because out there in the suburbs, when a rebellion is going on over here, you are standing there, you are not being aggressed upon, no one is attacking you, you are not being shot at, you are not being tear-gassed, and it is further true, as Chicago demonstrates, that we are now in a situation where the possibility of having a peaceful demonstration is continually jeopardized, and the era of peaceful demonstrations symbolized by 1961 to 1968 may very well be at an end, but that you can get from picking up the morning paper, and looking at Ocean Hill–Brownsville. You don't have to have me here to point that out to you.

ICHORD: There is still an element, Mr. Hayden. We don't know whether the statements are correctly—that they are correct quotes of your statement, and that was the question directed to you.

ASHBROOK: Yes, I brought up this point because my recollection of what he said was that he had never said anything of that type, and now, of course, under this circumstance—

HAYDEN: Those are not things of the same type. There is a difference.

Oh, forget it.

＊　　　＊　　　＊

CONLEY: Mr. Hayden, in connection with the testimony of Captain Kinney, this past spring in the Newark riots, he mentioned that a number of persons were associated with you in the Newark area prior to these particular riots, and among the people that he mentioned were a Carol Glassman, a Constance Brown, and a Corrina Fales. Were these people not also with you during the demonstrations which occurred in Chicago?

HAYDEN: Depends what you mean by with me. They were in Chicago.

CONLEY: Thank you, sir.

HAYDEN: They were not with me.

CONLEY: And, Mr. Hayden, is it not also a fact that the communication center for the National Mobilization in Chicago during the demonstrations and disturbances was manned by Carol Glassman?

HAYDEN: No. She was one of a good number of people who worked in the communications center.

CONLEY: And she is also the same Carol Glassman that attended the conference with you at Bratislava, Czechoslovakia, is she not?

HAYDEN: Yes.

CONLEY: Now, Mr. Hayden, is it not also true that two of your other associates, Constance Brown and Corrina Fales, were in Chicago and charged with pouring some type of acid on the lobby of a hotel there in Chicago?

HAYDEN: They were so arrested.

CONLEY: Thank you, sir.

HAYDEN: As far as I know. I mean, I wasn't able to be around at the time.

CONLEY: Sir, I have not asked you if you saw the act occur. I asked you if you were aware of the fact that they were—

HAYDEN: I wasn't even able to be anywhere in the city of Chicago, because of the police.

CONLEY: Now, Mr. Hayden, at the time of her arrest on this particular charge of dispensing acid or whatever it was on the floor of the hotel, Connie Brown had in her possession a paper containing the following words: "Hunting, slingshot, ball bearings, buy at sports shop. (With points on all sides, cans of lighter fluid, cans of spray paint, pieces of garden hose, cherry bombs, firecrackers.)"

Mr. Hayden, I hand you a photocopy of that particular document, and ask you if you have ever seen that before.

HAYDEN: No, I never have.

CONLEY: Do you recognize the handwriting on the document, sir?

HAYDEN: It is possible that I do, but I would not want to try to identify the handwriting.

CONLEY: Is the handwriting similar to the handwriting of Constance Brown?

HAYDEN: It could be. Why don't you ask her?

CONLEY: Mr. Hayden, was this type of information which is contained in this document in any way given to the people who participated in the demonstrations in Chicago by you, or any other members of the steering committee of the National Mobilization Committee?

HAYDEN: I told you that I didn't even know about this so-called document. It sounds like something Mayor Daley wrote, because it lists the kind of weapons that he said the demonstrators carried. I have already said that, or at least, I guess, in general I have already said, that no such things were

159

advocated officially or unofficially by anyone connected with the Mobilization.

CONLEY: My question to you—

HAYDEN: But what is your meaning?

CONLEY: My question to you, and I will repeat the question, because I think again you are reading more into my questions than I intend for you to read—

HAYDEN: I am just trying to speed the hearing up.

CONLEY: If you will, speed it up by listening to the question. The question again was, to your knowledge, did any member of National Mobilization steering committee or National Mobilization's staff put out information of this type?

HAYDEN: Didn't I just answer that?

CONLEY: I didn't ask you if you put out this document.

HAYDEN: No, the answer is no.

CONLEY: All right, sir, to your knowledge, did you hear any member of National Mobilization Committee advocating the purchase of or procuring of these type objects?

HAYDEN: No.

CONLEY: Mr. Hayden, the *Chicago Tribune* on May 22, 1968, in an interview with you by their reporter, Michael Killian, and this interview occurred in the offices of the National Mobilization Committee, 407 South Dearborn, Chicago, Mr. Killian quoted you as saying to him, "What we are seeking is instability."

And he stated that he overheard you taking a telephone call from New Jersey, in which you were overheard to say, "Fine. Send them on out. We will start the revolution now. Do they want to fight?"

Mr. Hayden, are these quotations correct?

HAYDEN: Not that I know of, sir. Killian, I believe, is an agent of the Chicago Police Department.

ICHORD: Mr. Hayden, you are saying you are not correctly quoted, Mr. Hayden?

HAYDEN: I don't believe that I said that. But I will tell you what the conversation was about, and again, it is an example of your extraordinary inability to think.

ICHORD: I don't see anything extraordinary about it at all, Mr. Hayden. It is very pertinent.

HAYDEN: I will be glad to explain to you why I was seeking instability.

Mr. Killian dropped by, and we talked, had a little interview for five or ten minutes, in which Mr. Killian asked me my views about universities, and whether they would shut down in the fall, and I said that I thought that there was a tremendous showdown coming on college campuses, for example, in California, between regents and businessmen and state legislatures on the one hand, and students and, increasingly, faculty on the other hand, and that this would lead to a crisis for the administration of the universities, to force them to side either with the tradition of the university or side with the state and business interests that control universities.

So you would have a situation in which one university administrator after another would either be fired or be retired, and I think that that is highly desirable: until the university situation straightens itself out, and that certainly is happening today at San Francisco State. It has happened at the University of California. It has happened at other universities. University administrators, university presidents, are being forced to choose what kind of university they want. One that serves business, or one that serves the traditions of academic freedom. And this instability of university administrations is a very important sign that times are changing.

And I would like to further point out, since I recall the conversation from memory, that the article again is an example of your extraordinary manipulation of information.

You choose the word "instability."

"What we are seeking is instability," in the context of a fourteen- or fifteen-inch article, which states pretty much exactly what I just said, but you didn't say that it referred to

161

college presidents, that it referred to college campuses, that it referred to anything but instability, as if instability was an end in itself.

CONLEY: Well, Mr. Hayden, we didn't aver either that it referred to the Democratic convention, did we?

HAYDEN: Not yet.

CONLEY: Let us go back. You say that the quotes are not accurate, that Mr. Killian has not properly quoted you, or not properly related what occurred, so the quotation, then, "What we are seeking is instability," taken, as you put it, from a larger contention, that is not an accurate quote?

HAYDEN: It is not an accurate quote, but the context is right there in the story. It is not Killian's fault, it is your fault.

CONLEY: Now, what about the second quotations which have been attributed to you?

HAYDEN: Those are an unbelievable joke.

CONLEY: Are you saying that Mr. Killian, representing the *Chicago Tribune*, has misquoted you specifically—

HAYDEN: Would you think that I would say in front of a *Chicago Tribune* reporter what was ascribed to me, unless it was said with a sense of humor right in front of his face, which could have been possible?

CONLEY: Are you saying that you could have said this, then?

HAYDEN: I certainly could have said it, but my question to you is what you think I meant by it.

ICHORD: The question is being put to you, Mr. Hayden.

CONLEY: The question is a very simple one, did you or did you not say it?

HAYDEN: To the best of my knowledge, I did not, but I could have.

CONLEY: All right, and if you could have, which means you really don't know whether you did or didn't?

HAYDEN: To the best of my knowledge, I did not, but I could have.

162

* * *

CONLEY: On page 1(b) of the September, 1968, *Challenge*, appears the following quote, attributed to you, sir.

Hayden said in Grant Park on Wednesday, "This city and the military machinery it has aimed at us won't permit us to protest in an organized fashion. Therefore, we must move out of this park in groups throughout the city, and turn this overheated military machine against itself. Let us make sure that if blood flows, it flows all over the city. If they use gas against us, let us make sure they use gas against their own citizens."

Mr. Hayden, my question is, did you make that statement on August 28, in Grant Park, at the band shell at approximately 2 P.M.?

HAYDEN: I made a statement similar to that, somewhat longer, at approximately that time, just after the police brought down the American flag, charged the crowd, and split Rennie Davis' scalp, and surrounded the demonstrators who were trying to nonviolently begin to march to the Amphitheater, led by David Dellinger.

At that time, with National Guardsmen standing on the roof of the museum, with gas coming down all over the park, with women and children trying to flee, I thought that we were in a cul de sac, surrounded by police, and my advice to the crowd was that it would be probably futile to expect to be able to march, even as far as the Conrad Hilton, and so people should separate, into groups of their friends, keep track of each other, because it was a very dangerous situation, and get out of the band shell area, and go back to the area of the Conrad Hilton, and the Loop, where we had been demonstrating for the previous three or four days.

And about the overheated military machinery, and the blood and the gas, I think I spoke at great length about that yesterday. My feeling all along was that the excessive military

163

preparations would lead to a state of insecurity for the city itself, and perhaps close the convention.

The convention would disrupt itself, not that we would invade it, but it would disrupt itself, and the thing that I did not want to happen on August 28 was for all of these demonstrators to be trapped down by the band shell, and wiped out by the police.

If they were going to be wiped out, if the convention was going to end with mass arrests or with mass gassing, or with mass bloodshed, my feeling was that it should take place in front of the Conrad Hilton, or in the Loop, and I hoped that if I was going to pass out from the gas, that it would waft its way into the fifteenth floor suite of Hubert Humphrey as well, which it did, and make him get the real sweet smell of democracy in Chicago, himself.

CONLEY: Mr. Hayden, if I may move back to something that we touched on earlier, and that is the article which appeared in the *Chicago Tribune*, under date of May 22, as I reread this article, you mentioned that you would be a fool to have made such a statement as was attributed to you in that article in the presence of a reporter for the *Tribune*.

HAYDEN: No.

CONLEY: Looking back through it, it appears that perhaps you left the room and went to another room, and that the reporter overheard your telephone conversation. Is that not what you read in that article?

HAYDEN: Listen, we are the most open organization you will ever investigate. That is why you can't catch us. We allowed any reporter or any spy from your committee or anywhere else to—

ICHORD: Mr. Hayden, let me explain to you. We are not trying to catch you, we are trying to find out the facts. You are not called before this committee to be punished or to be tried for any crime.

HAYDEN: That is a matter of interpretation.

ASHBROOK: Just a minute. On the matter of interpretation, I have listened very carefully to your very articulate defense of what you said or what you believe. Up to now you have talked about violence in the sense that to use your words, I believe, it might be defensible; in other cases, it might be the type of thing you would acquiesce in, but now, to be quite honest and frank, don't these words sound a little bit more like exhortations to violence than mere defensibility of violence or acquiescence in violence?

HAYDEN: No, sir, you had to have been there to understand what I was talking about. I was speaking while people, including myself, were gagging on tear gas, people were being carried off on stretchers, mobile hospitals were being set up before our eyes, police were being moved in in columns, and the violence was already around us.

It was hardly exhortation, except exhortation to move this whole situation over to the Hilton, and try to escape for as long as possible the obvious attack that was accelerating against us, right before our eyes.

This is on film. I am sure my speech is tape-recorded. You don't have to go into executive session to listen to it. And that is the kind of exhortation that it was, and I stand by it.

CONLEY: Mr. Hayden, moving to another subject, did you attend a meeting in Washington, D.C., on September 14 of this year, where further plans were made by the National Mobilization Committee, in connection with the upcoming elections? Did you attend such a meeting?

HAYDEN: Yes, I went to such a meeting. I naturally don't remember the exact date, but it was in Washington, about that time.

CONLEY: Reading from the minutes of that meeting, "Tom Hayden explained that the removal of Johnson to silence the antiwar sentiment underscores the strategic relationship of the war to the election and the candidates. He felt the outlined Davis proposal would successfully surface antiwar, antiracist sentiment, would allow moderates to participate in the rallies, and permit more militant action for the youth. He explained that the working classes wouldn't be changed by 'cooling it,' or by educational statements, but that the work with the armed forces during GI Week would prepare new ground. He argued against the conservative tone being injected into the meeting."

HAYDEN: That is fairly substantially my position at that time.

CONLEY: Now, isn't it a fact that at that particular meeting, three individuals whom we will identify as pacifists suggested that a nonviolent stance be assumed by the Mobilization Committee, and isn't it also true that you stood up and disagreed with this particular position? And I refer you specifically to your words in that, which are a "more militant action for youth."

HAYDEN: No, that doesn't mean that. That doesn't mean more militant in the sense of higher degree of militance, but continuing militance. More militant. It provides another, a further militant action for youth, as a follow-through from Chicago.

CONLEY: To me, sir, the better choice of words would have been "continuing militance."

HAYDEN: Well, you weren't the secretary, and we didn't expect HUAC, with its double and triple meanings, to examine the notes. But I would be glad to explain at great length, right now, everything that is meant by each and every word.

WATSON: At this point, when you advocate more militancy, granted, I am not of such a nature to construe that other than its simplest terms, and that means, to be more militant. The question I would like to know, since you are giving different interpretations now to such terms that you have used as "carry the torch," "shoot to kill," "more militancy," did you explain at that time what you meant by these terms?

HAYDEN: Yes.

166

WATSON: That they were not to be construed in the usual sense of their meaning?

HAYDEN: Well, that is a joke, the way you put the question.

WATSON: Well, now, you are giving them different meanings now, and all I am asking you is whether or not you explained at that time to those that you were urging to carry out these particular activities that you did not mean them to be literally taken, as an average person would construe them. That is—

HAYDEN: I think that people at the meeting could understand my terms. I argued that the elections should not be disrupted, that there should not be violence around polling places, that there should be demonstrations everywhere in the country, against the fraudulent choice put forward to the voters, of Nixon, Humphrey, and Wallace, that those people who don't feel represented, either because they can't agree with any of these three law-and-order candidates, or because they do not have the right to vote, which is true of most young people, should vote with their feet in the streets, should vote by having educational rallies on their campuses, and should try to again show the incoming President that he will be in the same hot water that Lyndon Johnson could only get out of by retiring from office, unless the Vietnam war is ended forthwith, period.

WATSON: Now I try it one more time to ask you the question, and see whether or not I can get an answer.

HAYDEN: I just answered your question.

WATSON: Did you at the time that you made the statement advocating more militancy on the part of youth explain to those who were listening to you that you did not mean for those words to be taken literally, but that you had an intellectual interpretation?

HAYDEN: No, I can't answer your question, because it is a loaded question. I said to those people—

WATSON: Yes, because I am trying to get the truth.

HAYDEN: I said to those people—the truth is what I just said, is what I said to those people.

WATSON: You did not explain to them.

HAYDEN: I just explained, very clearly—

WATSON: Thank you.

HAYDEN: —what the meaning of "militancy" was. That this kind of action was the only way that you could get moderate people, people with families, and jobs, together with the younger, more militant people, and it was a way to provide opportunities for more militant action of the kind that had been developing throughout the year, period.

CONLEY: Mr. Hayden, in addition to yourself at that meeting and Mr. Dellinger and Mr. Davis—and I am referring to the meeting in September in this city—were not also Mr. Harry Ring, of the Socialist Workers party, present?

HAYDEN: I believe he was. He came back. He was in disagreement. He is the Trotskyist I was telling you about. He came back to see what we were going to do next.

CONLEY: And was Mr. Lew Jones, of the Young Socialist Alliance?

HAYDEN: I believe that he was.

CONLEY: And Mr. Arnold Johnson, of the Communist party?

HAYDEN: I believe that he was. And the other people who were there, according to your list, were Gerald Schwinn, Tim McCarthy, Richard Ochs, Rod Robinson, Ken Katz, Irving Beinin, Emily Sack, Lenny Brody, Karl Baker, Tom Hayden, Alan Gross, Bob Kowollik, Judith Simmons, Dave Dellinger, Rennie Davis, Betty Hellman, Harry Ring, Lew Jones, Susan LaMont, Mike Maggi, Larry Seigle, Pat Grogan, John Tillman, Walter Reeves, John Wilson, Willy Louvallen, Irwin Gladstone, Josh Brown, Marcia Kallen, Abe Bloom, John Benson, Leland Sommers, Thomas L. Hayes, Gabrielle Edgcomb, Walter Schneir, Arnold Johnson, Marc Bedner, Richie Lesnik, Eric Weinberger, Bill Ayers, Terry Robbins, Joan

Campbell, Marilyn Lerch, Barbara Deming, Sidney Lens, Bradford Lyttle, Louis Kampf, Allan Brick, Trudi Schutz, Ron Young, Marty Teitel, Josie Teitel, Sandy Lutz, Arthur Waskow, Donna Gripe, Lee Webb, Jim Estes, Bernice Smith, Barbara Bick, Tibi Texler, Nona Stanton, Greg Sandow, Terry Gross, Ted Yarow, Helen Gurewitz, Richard M. Gold, and Edward Henderson.

Now what is the meaning of your selecting those three individuals? Why didn't you ask whether the members of the Fellowship of Reconciliation were there, or members from the Institute for Policy Studies were there, or representatives of the clergy?

ICHORD: Now the question, the witness is not being responsive. What is your question?

CONLEY: He has answered my question, Mr. Chairman. It is his dialogue.

ICHORD: It will be handed to the reporter, then.

CONLEY: He has identified who I wanted him to identify. Mr. Hayden, my next question to you is, did you attend a meeting of the National Lawyers Guild, 5 Beekman Street, New York City, on January 26, 1968?

HAYDEN: I attended a meeting in their offices. I am not sure there was a Guild meeting, and I don't know if that was exactly the date, but your informer, who wrote up the crazy notes, would probably at least be accurate about the date.

CONLEY: Now directing your attention to the minutes of that meeting, which I will be glad to supply to you—

HAYDEN: Minutes?

CONLEY: Yes, the minutes that were taken at that meeting. The minutes of a meeting to discuss setting up a legal committee for Chicago, January 26, 7:30 P.M., National Lawyers Guild Office, New York City.

My question, sir, is that the minutes taken at that meeting and distributed to the persons in attendance indicate that you said the following:

"Should have people organized who can fight the police. People who are willing to get arrested. No question that there will be a lot of arrests. My thinking is not to leave the initiative to the police."

Sir, did you make that statement?

HAYDEN: That statement I did not make, although I will elaborate the meaning of the statement, because I made one that was "strikingly similar," in your terms, and since it appeared today in *Life* magazine also, I have to set the record that your informer has created straight.

And I want to point out that this statement was made by an informer, and is not part of the minutes.

Now, the meaning of this statement that I made at the time was that we had to have legal and medical committees far in advance. We could not take, if we were responsible organizers of the Chicago action, we could not assume, or we could not avoid the problem of possible mass arrests and possible police brutality, and possible injunctions to keep us out of the city even before the convention started, and so it seemed necessary that we begin early in the year organizing at least lawyers and doctors, and I did not say that we should organize people to fight the police. We did not organize people to fight the police. I have always said that if you are attacked by a police officer, however, it is certainly your right, whether it is a legal right or not, to try to get away from him, to protect yourself, to exercise self-defense.

But I have said that at least ten times.

ICHORD: You mean, if a person is violating the law, and a policeman is enforcing the law?

HAYDEN: If a policeman is enforcing the law, he did not do it with a billyclub. If a policeman is making an arrest, as is his responsibility, that is responsible exercise of his function—unless it is a false arrest, of course—but what happened in Chicago was that there were more beatings than arrests.

There was a policy, in my opinion, to emphasize the beatings, rather than get bogged down by huge mass arrests, filling the jails, having to feed everybody, having to set up all the special courts, and the rest of it, and in that kind of situation, the policeman becomes the prosecutor, judge, jury, and executioner, on the spot, and in that case, crime in the streets is being carried on by the policeman.

CONLEY: Mr. Hayden, back to the original statement, did you or did you not make words to that effect?

HAYDEN: No. No, your informer missed.

WATSON: Now he did say that he made a statement strikingly similar to that.

HAYDEN: I was preempting what you would believe.

WATSON: Well, did you make a statement strikingly similar?

HAYDEN: I made a statement almost exactly of the nature that I just got through making.

WATSON: I see.

HAYDEN: It is for you to judge whether that is strikingly similar.

WATSON: I see. Well, perhaps you did use the terminology "strikingly similar." I ask you again, at that time, did you explain to those that you were urging to take such action against the police that you didn't literally mean them to do that?

HAYDEN: No, I said to them—

WATSON: Since you are giving moral interpretations.

HAYDEN: I said to them roughly what I just said.

WATSON: But did you explain to them that you didn't literally mean to them?

HAYDEN: No, I didn't explain anything as paternalistic and panderingly ridiculous and childish as that to grownup organizers, lawyers, and activists.

WATSON: In other words, you knew that they would not accept your words in the common understanding?

HAYDEN: You don't even know what you are talking about, Mr. Watson, because I didn't use the words—

WATSON: Well, I will agree with you that if most of them are like you, they will be speaking in foreign tongues and the interpretations indeed would be other than what a normal person would make under the circumstances.

DI SUVERO: Is the Congressman testifying now?

CONLEY: Mr. Hayden, in the *Esquire* magazine, December, 1968, edition, appears an article, "Will Tom Hayden Overcome?"

HAYDEN: It is a good question.

CONLEY: Referring you specifically to the first page and to the second column, and approximately one-half of the way down on that column, the following quotation, attributed to you, appears:

" 'It would be terrible,' he said, with an unerring sense of his own vincibility, 'if the revolution actually started and I was driving across the country.' "

Now, first of all, I will ask you if the quotation is accurate.

HAYDEN: I don't know, but again, you haven't read the entire thing, which he is trying to demonstrate what a great sense of humor I have, I gather. And he uses this, which didn't exactly tickle your sensibility, I noticed, so I guess I don't have a very good sense of humor. And since I don't remember offhand hilarious comments that I make from time to time, I don't know whether I said that or whether it is an invention of *Esquire*.

CONLEY: Now, Mr. Hayden, the National Council of SDS, of which you were formerly president, held a meeting at Boulder, Colorado, on October 10 through 12 of this year. A report of the major developments of that meeting was published in the SDS newspaper, *New Left Notes*, issue of October 18. And I quote to you from page 3 of that particular newspaper:

Much of the plenary discussion focused on the National Mobilization Committee and our relations to that group. Many persons felt that we should avoid any alliances with the MOBE, especially in light of the disastrous leadership provided by the Mobilization in Chicago. In addition to discussing the MOBE's politics, people also pointed out that marching to Washington would be just another march, which would accomplish nothing.

Now, Mr. Hayden, I ask you whether or not this was a slap at the leadership provided to National Mobilization by Mr. Dellinger, Mr. Davis, and yourself by the SDS organization?

HAYDEN: I was not at the meeting, but I am sure it was—it sounds like the Progressive Labor line. But I am sure that one of your experts on the varieties of leftism in America could supply you with a report about factional difficulties within SDS, within the Mobilization, and so forth.

I was not at the meeting. This is the first time that this statement was brought to my attention.

ICHORD: Are you still active in SDS, Mr. Hayden?

HAYDEN: I am not an officer of SDS. I remain in, and I speak on campuses often before SDS chapters, and I go perhaps to a meeting a year, or a meeting every two years, and I remain in somewhat frequent contact with their national office.

CONLEY: Mr. Hayden, you have previously testified that you wrote the preface to a book, *Mission to Hanoi*, which was published by Herbert Aptheker, a member of the Communist party, and is it also not a fact that in 1966 you served as an initial sponsor of the campaign committee for the same Herbert Aptheker to run for Congress as a Communist in the Twelfth Congressional District, Brooklyn?

HAYDEN: Yes. I thought that it was important. I didn't even support Aptheker. But I thought it was important that he be put on the ballot. I think it would be a good thing if members of the Communist party or any other party could legally participate in the American electoral system. It would then be less of a fraud.

ICHORD: You acted as his manager to get him on the ticket, and then didn't support him?

173

HAYDEN: I supported the idea that he should be on the ticket and allowed to run, but I didn't support him for Congress, because I am not personally that attracted to electoral politics, as you probably know from my previous testimony.

WATSON: No wonder he lost, if his manager didn't support him.

ICHORD: That is one of the difficult things I have in understanding you. How do you propose to elect a President, Mr. Hayden, by demonstrations to that effect?

HAYDEN: I never proposed to elect a President. Never proposed to elect a President.

CONLEY: Mr. Hayden, were you not also a speaker at the May Day rally, 1968, Los Angeles, California, sponsored by the Youth Section of the Communist party, U.S.A.?

HAYDEN: I agreed to speak, but then I did not. I did not go to California at that time.

CONLEY: And in addition to these other groups that I have indicated, have you not also worked with the Movement for the Independence of Puerto Rico, a violence-oriented Castroite group active in Puerto Rico and New York City?

DI SUVERO: Is the counsel testifying at the moment?

ICHORD: What was the question, Mr. Counsel? Read the question.

CONLEY: Has he worked with the Movement for the Independence of Puerto Rico?

HAYDEN: I have been in Puerto Rico once, at their invitation, and appeared, but did not speak, at a rally given by their leader, Juan Maria Bras, and though I am not that closely—I don't know that much in detail about the politics of the Puerto Rican Independence Movement, I would be proud to say that I supported the struggle of the people in Puerto Rico against the draft, against the Vietnam war, and for the development of Puerto Rico as an independent country, and I support organizations that work for that end, and as far as I

174

know, the Movement for Puerto Rican Independence is the leading organization of that kind.

It is not clear to me that it was a violent or violence-oriented organization, as you put it, but obviously they are sympathetic to the Cuban Revolution, and obviously I am sympathetic to the Cuban Revolution.

CONLEY: This trip that you made to Puerto Rico was in April of 1967, was it not?

HAYDEN: I don't remember the exact date, but it was in the spring, 1967. For about a week, or five days.

CONLEY: Mr. Hayden, is it your present aim to seek the destruction of the present American democratic system?

HAYDEN: That is a joke.

CONLEY: I am asking you, sir.

HAYDEN: Well, I don't believe the present American democratic system exists. That is why we can't get together, to straighten things out. I mean, I believe that you have destroyed the American democratic system, by the existence of a committee of this kind.

CONLEY: Well, let us use the word "system," then, let us take the words "American" and "democratic" out of it, and let us just call it the system. Is it your aim to destroy the present system?

HAYDEN: What do you mean by "destroy?"

CONLEY: To overturn it.

HAYDEN: What do you mean by "overturn it?"

CONLEY: To do away with it.

HAYDEN: What do you mean by "do away with it?" By what means?

CONLEY: I am asking you, sir.

HAYDEN: No, you asked me whether it was my aim.

CONLEY: I am asking you if that is your aim, sir.

HAYDEN: The question is too ambiguous.

ICHORD: Getting into the field of political philosophy, the

175

witness has testified at length as to his philosophy, Mr. Counsel. It would be very difficult for the Chair to direct an answer to the question.

CONLEY: Mr. Hayden, I have one final question for you. Ambrose Bierce, in his *Devil's Dictionary*, defines a conspirator as "Someone who finds it necessary to write down everything for his enemy to find." Mr. Hayden, you were clever enough not to be carrying any names or addresses on your person, or any slips of paper, at the time of the events in Chicago. However, in the purse of Miss Constance Brown was a complete list of names and addresses which were purportedly prepared by you.

And I would ask you, sir, don't you think that the young people who follow you in these various movements should take a second look at you, before they place their lives and their responsibilities in the hands of you?

HAYDEN: Shit.

ICHORD: The witness will please be seated.

HAYDEN: I thought that was the final question.

ICHORD: The Chair directs the witness to be seated.

WATSON: Mr. Chairman, may I make this point? I know there are advocates of free speech, and the witness is one of them, but I happen to be one who will not tolerate any such language as that. We have ladies in this room, and I shall not tolerate it, and if it is necessary for me to ask the police to arrest a man for such disorderly language as that, I shall do so. I am not going to tolerate language such as that, in the presence of ladies.

HAYDEN: Well, will you tolerate a question of the indecent kind that was just made by your own counsel?

ICHORD: Let us continue with the hearings, and the committee can let stand in the record, and take that under advisement, at the proper time.

Let the witness be admonished that this is a committee of Congress, consisting of duly elected members, and this committee is a legislative arm of Congress, and there are ways of enforcing proper order before the committee. There is such a thing as, as I have stated to the witness before, to his attorney, as contempt.

ICHORD: Let us proceed with the questioning again. We have gotten along very well here thus far. The witness has testified relatively freely compared to other witnesses appearing before the committee.

Rephrase your question, Mr. Counsel.

CONLEY: Mr. Chairman, that completes our questioning.

ASHBROOK: Mr. Hayden, I have listened very intently to your description of the events in Chicago, your opinions on that, and I would admit one area is not completely clear.

Sometimes I get the impression that you indicate what happened in Chicago was unfortunate, a travesty, and so forth. Other times, I get the indication you believe, at least it comes through in what you say, that Chicago was valuable, in that it demonstrated certain things, brought to the surface what you consider to be unfair treatment, some of the wrongs of the political processes.

There is somewhat of a dilemma here. I would like to have for the record whether you think now, looking back to the Chicago convention, what happened was good, bad, or helpful to your movement.

You have talked kind of from both sides. I would like to know which is your honest point of view.

HAYDEN: I have talked both sides, because we are going to win either way, Mr. Ashbrook. We would have won if it would have been safe and secure for 200,000 rank-and-file people, ordinary people to come to Chicago and protest. That would have had a profoundly discrediting effect on the Democratic party as it ratified the war in Vietnam, and nominated Hubert Humphrey, and would have defeated the Democratic party by the alienation of its grassroots base.

Since that was not allowed, because of the failure of the

city to grant permits, since that was not allowed because there was too much jeopardy facing anybody with a family or job, and since they didn't come to Chicago, we won in a different way, by exposing the brute nature that underlies the supposedly democratic two-party system.

I would have preferred to win the first way, but the second way was a tremendous victory of a kind for the young people in this country, people who are not voters, people who are never polled by Gallup or Harris, but people who watch on television, and do not identify with young people like the young Nixon girls and David Eisenhower, but identify with the young people who are in the streets of Chicago, and watch very carefully.

If you think that you have had militant people before you in these hearings, you have yet to see what the seven- and eight-year-olds are going to bring you over the next five or ten years.

You have taught them very well to have no respect for your authority, by what has happened in the city of Chicago. And that is a victory in the sense that committees like yourselves are now through. You exist only formally; you exist officially, but you have lost all authority, and when a group of people who have power lose their authority, then they have lost. You have lost, period.

That is why I have been quiet. That is why these hearings aren't disrupted, that is why no one comes to these hearings to picket any more, because the job has been done against HUAC, and the job has virtually been done against politicians.

ICHORD: And you say you are eventually going to do the job against the whole United States?

HAYDEN: Politicians of the kind like Dean Rusk, Lyndon Johnson, Richard Nixon, Hubert Humphrey, these people are in a sense already finished, because they can't exercise any authority, they have no respect from wide sections of the American people.

Richard Nixon does not even believe that Beatles albums should be played. He believes that drugs are the curse of American youth.

ICHORD: Of course, Mr. Hayden, you are very fortunate to have the protection of the First Amendment rights. Do you think that if you had performed the acts that you have performed, and such things that you have said, in North Vietnam, in behalf of America, that you wouldn't be shot on the spot? Do you think you would be given the same amount of liberty, guarantees of First Amendment rights which you have been given?

HAYDEN: Mr. Ichord, I don't consider that I have that much freedom. Is it freedom to sit here and under penalty of going to jail, if I don't talk to you, and express my opinions over and over, in a committee chamber of this sort, knowing full well that the opinions are hot air, they have no effect on your ears, they will not change a thing? If that is freedom, that is a very inadequate definition of freedom.

ICHORD: You have indeed a very strange philosophy, sir. You say that you don't care about electing a President. You don't care about a President at all. What kind of government do you want?

HAYDEN: I want a democratic government. My views on that are spelled out—not so very well, perhaps, certainly not in my opinion, but they are spelled out in exhaustive detail in all kinds of things that I have written, which I would be glad to submit to you, but I think that the question at this point would be a little bit redundant.

ASHBROOK: If I could possibly crystallize what you have said, and going back to the original question, it would be, as I understand it, from your point of view, that you would have preferred to have another approach in Chicago, and from your point of view, this was pushed upon you, but once it happened, it did pinpoint some of your criticisms of the democratic process, and as such, probably helped in the overall situation. I gather this is what you are saying.

But from what you are saying about the democratic processes, you are reasonably clear, from what you say—at least it comes through to me—that this was not good for the democratic processes in this country, at least from your point of view, but would be good from the point of view of those who think the democratic processes are in an Establishment, a white majority, etc., and won't work.

Would that be a reasonable summation of what you have said? Trying to differentiate between your point of view and our point of view? What happened in Chicago did not help the democratic process in this country?

HAYDEN: From your point of view. From my point of view, it did.

ASHBROOK: Well, then, maybe that is why I have a hard time understanding your statement, which is made in the *New York Times,* on September 1, 1968, from Downers Grove, Illinois, where it quoted you directly as saying, by John Kifner, their reporter, "We are going to create little Chicagos everywhere the candidates appear."

If what happened in Chicago was bad, and, of course, some of what you have said indicates that it was bad, it should be avoided, it was unfortunate, and once happening, you had to derive some benefit for those who want change, now you are in a position of saying that nevertheless, you want little Chicagos, 200, 300 Chicagos throughout the country. Is that a fair statement?

HAYDEN: Yes. I wanted, and many of us wanted, the energy and momentum of the Chicago demonstration to be carried back to the communities where the demonstrators came from, and the criticism of the Democratic party, criticism of the false choices in the elections, criticism of the fact that there was no way to vote for peace in the 1968 elections, to be made very clear in these local communities, and I wanted the people to go back from Chicago and interpret what happened in Chicago to students in high schools and colleges, and their neighbors, and I wanted demonstrations to occur whenever candidates came to speak, and there were some demonstrations around the country when candidates came to speak, and we wanted Election Day demonstrations, and there were some Election Day demonstrations.

ASHBROOK: Well, then, I would be wrong in assuming, when you say you wanted to create little Chicagos in the country, you are talking from the standpoint of demonstrations, where I guess I was thinking you meant that you wanted the police to be hitting people on the head, and that kind of thing.

HAYDEN: Well, it takes two to do that. It takes an initiator, and I think that police learned from Chicago to temporarily pull back, in some local situations, because they wanted to get Hubert Humphrey elected President.

ASHBROOK: The police wanted to?

HAYDEN: No, not the police, but the people who order the police. Certainly the police didn't want Hubert Humphrey elected President.

ASHBROOK: On one other point, I think it is very important, because we are looking at all the statements in the context of what you have said, what your meaning is, to what you have said, and I think you pointed out very articulately that you do have some different meaning than what many of us might think would come from that; that is a good example there; but from your own words—and I know quite often you have been misquoted; I can understand that, everybody is misquoted—but from your own words, on June 15, 1968, issue of *Ramparts*, page 40, where it says, "Two, Three, Many Columbias," that is the heading, it says, "by Tom Hayden," you state the following: You are going to say I take it out of context. I will suggest the whole article be placed in the record.

But you say,

Columbia opened a new tactical stage in the resistance movement which began last fall, from the overnight occupation of buildings to permanent occupation, from mill-ins to the creation of revolutionary committees, symbolic civil disobedience to barricaded resistance. Not only are these tactics already being duplicated on other campuses, but they are sure to be surpassed by even more militant tactics. In the future, it is conceivable that students will threaten the destruction of buildings as a last deterrent to police attacks. Many of the tactics learned can also be applied in smaller hit-and-run organizations between strikes. Raids on the offices of professors doing weapons research could win substantial support among students, while making the university more blatantly repressive.

I would have to say, when I observe this, and other statements you have made, most of the tenor that I get out of them is a call to more militant action. I know you have defined what you mean by "militant."

Here you are talking about taking over buildings, you are talking about hit-and-run organizations between strikes, raids on offices, maybe we get back to the old semantic argument we had yesterday, of what "attack" means, of what "pinning delegates in the convention" means, what the statement "anything to stop this farce" means, of what "guerrillas" means, but it seems to me that this sets the stage or sets the atmosphere for the confrontations with the policy, a confrontation with the authority everywhere, which many of us feel might have happened in Chicago, and might have been one of the causes.

Now I hand you the whole article. I assure you I didn't take it out of context, because I have read it three or four times, and those words that you state, isn't it fair for any reasonable person, possibly even a member of Congress, to feel that you are advocating more militant action, up to and including illegal action?

HAYDEN: Well, we would disagree on whether it is illegal action.

ASHBROOK: To take over a building?

HAYDEN: I think it is unconstitutional for the Columbia Board of Trustees to be appointed for life.

ASHBROOK: But not to prevent students from going to class?

HAYDEN: I think it is illegal and unconstitutional for scientists to make weapons which are banned by the Geneva Agreements and other international treaties, and to make them on university campuses.

I think that in the whole area of student riots and welfare, students are threatened in a way that gives them less actual legal and civil rights than convicts in a penitentiary have.

My views on this are extremely thoroughly written down. I don't believe that there is a democratic machinery on the campus. I don't believe the draft represents democratic machinery, and as long as there is no democratic machinery, then young people will either have to capitulate in the status quo, or have to find ways to resist it, and I don't really advise that people find illegal ways to resist it, because I think that the authorities are going to start putting people away.

Most of my friends are on their way to jail, for one thing or another. Most of the young leaders in this country, in the movements, many of them unknown to you, many of them unknown to me, are facing prison sentences already, so I beg to differ with the idea that I advocate illegal action, but I do advocate action that could bring a university to a halt, as the actions of the students and faculty at San Francisco State have brought that university to a halt, to try to straighten the university out.

ASHBROOK: Mr. Hayden, maybe we would disagree on the term, but it seemed to me from what you have said that that comes very close to anarchy.

183

HAYDEN: Well, we are living in a state of anarchy. When a young man is faced by a draft board, the average age of its members are fifty-eight, one-fifth of those members are seventy-three years old, there is no mechanism for that young person to avoid intolerable choices, either of fighting in a war that he doesn't want to fight in, or copping out and letting some Puerto Rican or young black person or poor working-class person fight for him, then isn't that a state of anarchy facing that individual, rather than a state of law?

He has no recourse. He has no machinery, and that is the situation facing all young people in this country, and it is a situation that I could describe in great detail, in other spheres besides the draft.

WATSON: Mr. Hayden, I believe you stated in summation that we are going to lose, referring to the present generation, the Establishment.

HAYDEN: No, I just meant HUAC has lost its authority. That is why no one pickets here any more.

WATSON: I see. Of course, perhaps some of us may assign other reasons as to why they no longer picket, but—

HAYDEN: I hope you don't think it is the police.

WATSON: Oh, of course not. You have demonstrated that you have no fear or respect for police authority. But did I not understand—

HAYDEN: Not when it is used in the way that you are using it to protect your so-called democracy.

WATSON: Did I understand you to say that the system, or whatever it is, this generation, we are going to lose?

HAYDEN: I think that politicians like Dean Rusk, Lyndon Johnson, Richard Nixon, Hubert Humphrey, and anybody else I might have listed before and now forgotten have lost their authority with wide sections of the American people. I said that. I said that HUAC has lost its authority.

WATSON: And that you—

HAYDEN: And that you can't retain it by having a younger

chairman, or being more reasonable, because that doesn't deal with the fundamental questions.

ICHORD: Mr. Hayden, some of the newspaper columnists have stated that you and your group were very instrumental in the election of Richard Nixon. Doesn't that somewhat frustrate you, with your feeling toward Richard Nixon, if those columnists are accurate in their assessment?

HAYDEN: No. I think that the election of Richard Nixon, in a sense, shows that the country will continue to run down, until people decide to straighten it out. You know, it doesn't really matter to me whether Hubert Humphrey or Richard Nixon is president of the United States.

WATSON: You didn't say earlier that you and those of your thinking were going to ultimately win?

HAYDEN: Well, I think we will at least outlive you.

(Laughter.) Probably much of our time will be spent in penitentiaries. I think that we are more than an existential or romantic movement, however; I think we are a calculating movement, a political movement, and we are trying to make this country a better country, and we expect that—we have every reason to believe that we have some chance to be successful in that effort.

WATSON: So your ultimate objective is to make this country a better country. You made that statement.

HAYDEN: Well, yes, I just made that statement.

WATSON: And you have, I believe, a lot of, or several comments in support of the so-called Walker Report.

HAYDEN: Not quite. I don't quite agree with the Walker Report.

WATSON: You don't quite. But some parts of it, you do, as I recall earlier, you said that it condemned this—

HAYDEN: It has a lot of evidence of what happened in Chicago between the police and demonstrators, that I think is accurate evidence. Solid evidence.

WATSON: Well, in this report on page 49, I would like to

185

read a paragraph from it, which the report says is a typical yippie flier, and it reads as follows:

"Who says the rich white Americans can tell the Chinese what is best? How dare you tell the poor that their poverty is deserved? If f—— nuns"—and you know what I mean.

HAYDEN: What do you mean, Mr. Watson?

WATSON: —"Laugh at professors"—

HAYDEN: What do you mean, Mr. Watson?

WATSON: I will give you credit for being intelligent enough to arrive at an interpretation yourself.

"—disobey your parents. Burn your money. You know life is a dream, and all our institutions are manmade illusions, effective because you take the dream of reality. Break down the family, church, nature, city, economy, turn life into an art form, and theater of the soul, and a theater of the future. The revolutionary is only an artist. What is needed is a generation of people who are freaky, crazy, irrational, sexy, angry, irreligious, childish, and mad. People who burn draft cards, burn high school and college degrees, people who say 'to hell to your goals.' People who lure the youth with music, pot, and acid, people who redefine the normal, people who break with the status–royal-title–consumer game, people who have nothing material to lose but their flesh, and finally, the white youth of America have more in common with Indians plundered than they do with their own parents. Burn your houses down, and you will be free."

That is a typical yippie flier, those associated with you in this movement in Chicago, and this, in your judgment, is the way to have a better America?

HAYDEN: I think that beautiful sentiments are expressed in that statement, and I wish that you could understand them, Mr. Watson.

WATSON: Fine, that wraps it up real well.

About Tom Hayden

Tom Hayden attended the University of Michigan from 1957 to 1961 and returned there in 1962 through part of 1964 as a graduate student and as an instructor. He has taught political science at Rutgers University and has published two books, *Rebellion in Newark* on the conditions in Newark at the time of the rebellion, and *The Other Side,* with Staughton Lynd, about North Vietnam. He is presently engaged in organizing radical education in the San Francisco Bay area.

599

5351